Endorsements

Deborah's positive energy is so contagious; I am often in a totally blissful state after our sessions. I love that her story is so accessible and that she freely admits she has come from a place of discouragement and despair similar to the one so many of us are wrestling with. Deborah's is a story of hope—living proof of what is possible.

—Megan

As a result of Deborah's coaching, I was finally able to forgive my father for all the abuse I received from him and free myself from feeling that I was 'not enough.' Through my work with Deborah, I came to see that it was my father's feelings of inadequacy that kept him from loving himself or anyone else, not any insufficiency in me. Once I was able to let go of my bitterness, I could thank him for the gift of life and for the role he played in learning to love myself. I've been able to help others find release from past pain and self-imposed limitations by sharing my lesson freely. I so appreciate Deborah's presence in my life.

—Caroline

Deborah's no wizard behind a curtain. She's the real deal. Her wisdom, sensitivity, and ability to listen were essential to my transformation. People who've watched me change know the work I've done was not an accident. Deborah has been a blessing in my life. I'm excited about all the unexplored possibilities still before us.

—Diana

When I look at the work I've done with Deborah, perhaps the greatest value lies in seeing myself differently. Her ability to facilitate my self-discovery through provocative questions and gentle guidance allowed me to accept that I don't have to have all the answers.

—Anne

Deborah is a night-light. She shines light on the dark places. She walks with you, she holds your hand, but she won't, she can't, do the work for you. If you have the courage and commitment to get up and walk—to do the hard work of changing—your journey will be incredibly rewarding. Deborah will help you strengthen your 'core' quicker than any ab exercise out there.

—Lori

Deborah is insightful, intuitive, warm, and welcoming—a tremendous asset to anyone's journey. Your life will be enlightened and blessed by walking with her.

—Sarah

Deborah has an uncanny ability to listen. She knows what I'm trying to communicate and connects me with something much deeper than I'd find on my own. She handles every conversation with respect and compassion.

—Sam

I find Deborah's approach to be unique. Her great advantage is the ability to bring together a strong professional background, a deeply spiritual perspective, and a personal character born out of overcoming her own challenges and leveraging her life experiences to support others on their Journeys to Wholeness.

—Lily

Everything Deborah does, she does wholeheartedly and with great professionalism. Her calm, articulate presence and deep intuition are among the great gifts she shares with her clients.

—Betty

Deborah's ability to get to the core of an issue just takes my breath away. Her insight distills things down to the simple truth—a truth clear enough for you to work with and through. She provides tools to help me navigate and reconnect with my authentic self. Don't be surprised if you start by focusing in one area of your life, only to make deeper, more-profound discoveries and changes in other aspects of your life as well.

—Cecilia

As an aspiring professional coach, I reached out to Deborah to augment my certification training and help me get focused. She met my objectives and so much more. The most surprising and valuable result of our work together was a significant transformation within myself. Changing so many parts of myself from the inside out really solidified the reason that I want to be a professional coach. The feeling of a deep, personal transformation is so uniquely profound, words cannot come close to fully describing the lasting impact. Deborah helped me rediscover that feeling of hope and endless possibilities inside myself which so inspires me to partner with my clients in doing the same.

—Mark

Deborah listens in a way that is hard to explain. She is extraordinarily intuitive and asks penetrating questions that helped me get past how much my body weighed and begin to see the weight on my spirit.

—Lisa

My journey in search of self over several decades has involved many modalities and an eclectic mix of spiritual paths. My breakthroughs with Deborah revealed a beneficial new path through which I continually grow in my ability to recognize, respect, heal, and transcend the fear-based aspects of my ego. By learning to let go of my anxiety and self-doubts, I have been able strengthen and expand my sense of self within and as an essential contributor to the unfolding of the universe. A truly amazing and rewarding journey that I never expected!

—Sandra

My therapist recommended Deborah's services when life handed me a few extra helpings of uncertainty with a divorce, a career change, and more. Deborah's loving partnership and insight helped me get off my own incessantly spinning hamster wheel. She helped me discover the abundant power within me and manifest my full potential. With her support, I found the courage to pursue two lifelong dreams: moving to India and writing my first book. Both felt unattainable one year ago today, and yet, with Deborah's guidance, I've begun to live the life I dreamed of. She's a life coach miracle worker! I am forever grateful.

—Janice

Deborah and I met while completing the extensive iPEC coach certification. We've stayed in touch, and recently she offered me a complimentary coaching session. What I gained from that one session is priceless. She helped me think through the reasons I was putting off important actions that would move my business forward. I am seeing instant benefits from the action I took the very next day. Deborah has keen insight, is a great listener, and has a tremendous sense of creativity in helping you find the answers you seeks. She is one of the best in the industry!

—Kathy

I was drawn to Deborah from the moment I met her. Her brilliance and insight are undeniable. Deborah has a special gift. You talk to her for just a moment and you are changed forever. With a wealth of knowledge, she takes you deeper, helps you find meaning and insight, and gives you tools to be your very best in all areas of life.

—Kim

One of the byproducts of my strong sense of responsibility is that I don't laugh nearly often enough. But when coaching with Deborah, quite often I experience spontaneous, therapeutic laughing spells. When she helps me cut through my mind fog and excuses to see the truth, all I can do is laugh with delight! Hire Deborah as your coach; get greater clarity and learn to laugh more!

—Sylvia

When Deborah hired me to create a photo collection to promote her new book and radio show, I wanted to gain a deeper understanding of her work as a life coach. So I scheduled a complimentary coaching session with her. She began by explaining how the session would unfold. She then guided me through a brief two-minute relaxation exercise to help me detach from any worries over the past or future so I could clear my mind and be fully present. The beauty of coaching by phone was the absolute privacy and comfort of being in my own space. For the focus of our session, Deborah invited me to choose one thing I wanted to accomplish in the next thirty days that I didn't think I could. With her gentle guidance, I realized I can accomplish much more than I give myself credit for. Together, we made a plan. That one thing I wanted to accomplish but couldn't? Done in a matter of days! I highly recommend Deborah's services as a life coach. She has an energy that is calming and full of love and light!

—Susan

Working with Deborah has been an eye-opener! In the past, when I encountered conflict, large or small, I always took it personally and had a hard time letting it go. Through our coaching, it became clear to me that most of what the other person was saying and doing wasn't really about me but about the host of life experiences and other variables that person brought to the situation. When Deborah helped me "get curious" about why I was feeling the way I was, I gained a new perspective that greatly reduced my stress. Deborah's insight, support and honest observations will help you find the answers you seek. I am forever grateful for the knowledge and confidence she helped me discover within myself.

—Rebecca

I knew Deborah before she became a professional life coach. I've been amazed at how she has changed her life. When I decided it was time to begin making decisions about the next phase of my life, I knew immediately that Deborah was the person I wanted to work with. Her personal and professional experiences help her guide clients through coaching in a way that is individualized and delightfully eye-opening. Her warmth and sensitivity are immediately apparent, even over the phone. With gentle encouragement and permission, she will guide you through an examination of your life, including difficult experiences. She will help you gain insight from your past choices and then explore possibilities for moving forward in less encumbered ways. When you work with Deborah, your life will take on new meaning and your potential will be limitless!

—Chris

The work I did with Deborah continues to change my life. While I have learned many valuable lessons from her, the greatest was the deep insight that is available to me when I listen to and learn from my own inner wisdom. Her intuition, discernment, and encouragement have taught me to trust my own intuition, creating new paths and possibilities for my life. One of Deborah's great gifts is helping others respect and connect with their inner guidance and through that connection form a deeper, more meaningful bond with the collective wisdom and energy of all.

—Ryan

CHOOSE YOUR ENERGY:
CHANGE YOUR
Life!

CHOOSE YOUR ENERGY:
CHANGE YOUR
Life!

When you fall in love with yourself,
everything else falls into place

DEBORAH JANE WELLS

BALBOA.
PRESS

A DIVISION OF HAY HOUSE

Balboa Press books may be ordered through booksellers or by contacting:

Balboa Press
A Division of Hay House
1663 Liberty Drive
Bloomington, IN 47403
www.balboapress.com
1-(877) 407-4847

Printed in the United States of America.

ISBN: 978-1-4525-7319-9 (sc)
ISBN: 978-1-4525-7321-2 (hc)
ISBN: 978-1-4525-7320-5 (e)
Library of Congress Control Number: 2013907690
Balboa Press rev. date: 6/11/2013

With a Foreword by
Liz Phillips Fisch, *CPC, PCC, ELI-MP, M.Ed., Vice President,
Institute for Professional Excellence in Coaching (iPEC)*

Dedication

For my Sources, human and Divine, with eternal love and gratitude for the gift of life. Your precious legacy made possible everything that followed—my personal Journey to Wholeness and the joy of sharing my message of hope and possibilities with the world.

- *Gladys "Gladdie" Elizabeth Aust Wells*
- *John Wesley Wells, Sr.*
- *Grace Marion Adams Aust*
- *Harry Aust*
- *Kathryn Grace Drumheller Reichenbach Wells*
- *Eli Kirschner Wells*

And for my beloved life companions, human and feline, whose love, respect, curiosity, compassion, and gratitude infuse each moment of my life with faith, hope, prosperity, peace, and joy. Your very existence enriches my ability to reveal and advance the highest good for all, in all, through all.

- *Wilson Ray Abney*
- *Matthew Dungan Abney*
- *Anne Elizabeth Barton*
- *SiddhaLee*
- *Mortimer*
- *Maisy Jane*

Contents

Illustrations

You may download larger full-color versions of all illustrations by signing up for my Book Insider Club at www.tiny.cc/djwbookclub.

When you fall in love with yourself,
everything else finally falls into place,
with beauty, power, and grace.
When you release the illusion of fear
and embrace the truth of love,
you will know in each moment
who you are and Whose you are.
That, my dear friends,
is more than enough.
It is everything.
—Deborah Jane Wells

Foreword

My library is filled with self-help books, stories of personal transformation, and books about coaching, leadership, and psychology. The book you are about to read combines elements of all of these genres and will lead you on a personal journey to self-understanding, self-acceptance, and self-love. Lest you think that sounds "self-ish," let me assure you that, as Deborah explains very effectively in her "Lesson of the Oxygen Mask" in part I, chapter 2, those qualities are essential for every aspect of your life, including your relationships with others. The best gift that you can give yourself—and others—is the gift of self-love, which leads to an authentic life of truly expressing yourself in all that you do.

I first met Deborah at her last live weekend of training to become a life coach. As a trainer, curriculum developer, and researcher at the Institute for Professional Excellence in Coaching (iPEC), I am privileged to meet, and be inspired by, hundreds of students each year. These students take the iPEC training they receive to coach with different focuses (life purpose, relationships, wellness, etc.) in many different areas (corporate, small business, healthcare, athletics, etc.). I can't say that I remember them all—though I try to—but Deborah was one who stood out for me. In fact, drawn by her message of "falling in love with yourself," I hired her as my own personal coach and have been working with her, over a period of many months, exploring the concepts contained in this book.

This work is powerful and transformational. Deborah is a guide with ultimate credibility—not only has she mastered coaching skills, but she's wise and intuitive, she's been on this path herself, and she freely and generously desires to share the wisdom she's learned on that journey. I marveled, as I read though the book, at how much I did *not* know about the details of Deborah's story;

this is a testament to her complete objectivity in our sessions and her purpose, throughout those sessions, of focusing entirely on me and my growth. The Discovery Framework that she so eloquently describes in this book is something that we've worked on extensively. It was powerful for me, even after months of working on "getting to know" my personal board of directors and the factors that feed my soul, to read the comprehensive explanation she sets forth here.

One gift that cannot be shared in a book is the gift of Deborah's intuitive hits—often, she knows what I'm feeling, and why, even before I do. Having her as a partner on my journey has made the path richer and deeper. Through her book, we all now have her words and wisdom available any time we want a guide to living an authentic life filled with love, respect, curiosity, compassion, and gratitude.

Wishing you the best on your personal journey,

Liz Phillips Fisch, *CPC, PCC, ELI-MP, M.Ed., Vice President, Institute for Professional Excellence in Coaching (iPEC)*

Preface

When your birth includes a near-death experience, you know you are in for a wild ride. A fifty-five-year roller coaster of triumph and burnout led to finding my life purpose more than five decades later. Mine is a story of hope. Yours can be too.

As a life coach, organization transformation consultant, Reiki master, artist, author, and broadcast personality, I have pursued a lifelong passion for the transformative power of love. I help individuals and organizations learn to harness that power to step into their greatness.

When we choose fear as our fuel, any of us—individuals and organizations alike—can become stuck in the "hamster wheel" approach to life. Trapped by the mistaken belief that busyness is the same as purpose, we can't stand the way we're living but feel powerless to change.

As we work together, my clients discover what I discovered: when you fall in love with yourself, everything else falls into place, personally and professionally. Choosing love as your core energy automatically enhances every aspect of your life: your perceptions, opportunities, relationships, and priorities. You get unstuck, reclaim your personal power, and recapture your zest for living, moving yourself forward into a life you love. When love transforms your relationship with yourself, it transforms your personal life, your work, and the world.

Instead of choosing to live as a victim of circumstance, consider embracing the power of loving yourself unconditionally through insights, encouragement, clear strategies, and practical tools built on

- my personal journey, including a sustained eighty-pound

weight loss, freedom from a ten-year bout of debilitating depression, and finding my purpose guiding others on their journeys;

- living in flow, a fluid Journey to Wholeness grounded in who you are being *not* what you are doing;
- the Discovery Framework that grew out of my experience, including core energy, sensory balance, and your personal board of directors; and
- Lessons in Living inspired by the journeys of my clients.

What's love got to do with it? Everything!

The remaining sections of this preface remove some artificial barriers from your path so that you will be free to fully embrace and benefit from all the possibilities this book offers. In doing this work with others, I have encountered three common areas of misperception.

Easy Does It

You may be saying to yourself, "It's easy for her to be optimistic. She's a professional life coach with a weekly radio show and a published book. She has no idea how hard it is to make significant lasting change." Believe me, I *do* know, as will become abundantly clear when you read my own story of transformation in chapter 1.

I'm far from finished learning that lesson. Life continues to send me reminders of how hard or easy change can be. It's all a matter of the thoughts and tools I use to fuel myself. Take writing this book as an example.

Even once I had set my intention, this book was not written overnight. Even though I was already doing lots of polished, persuasive speaking and writing on the subject, this book was not written overnight. Even though I spent much of my thirty-year consulting career writing about transformation for a living, *this book was not written overnight.*

Though writing a book made complete sense *intellectually* (head response), every time I thought about the scope, complexity, and importance of the project, not to mention the greater vulnerability that such increased visibility could bring, I would begin hyperventilating at the sheer magnitude of what was before me (heart response).

I followed my own advice; I didn't force myself to do anything before I felt ready. I respected my intuition in the form of my energy for the project and set my intention to open myself wide to knowing what the best approach would be—content, design, flow, and timing.

One of my favorite tools to employ when I begin to block myself with the perceived enormity of a new project is to ask, "What if this is going to be much easier than I think?" Having opened the door to that delightful possibility, I immediately anchor it more deeply as an affirmation: "Writing this book is going to be easy, fast, and fun. Effortless, joyful, creative, rewarding. Just the ticket to help my practice and myself grow in new directions and touch more lives in support of the highest good for all."

Remembering that early success fosters flow, I started with the parts I knew would be relatively simple. The constructive fuel from that fast sense of accomplishment helped me continue to flow right on into the more complex elements, one word, one sentence, one paragraph, one page, one section at a time.

Then I let the project simmer on the back burner while I kept moving forward in other areas of my life. I checked back in occasionally, took the lid off the stockpot, gave it a stir and a taste. I added some new ingredients (rendered some new diagrams, wrote a few paragraphs or another chapter, incorporated and adapted some writing I'd just done for another purpose) and adjusted the seasonings (flipped the order of sections, changed the formatting for greater clarity, tweaked some language for greater impact). Then I put the lid back on and let it keep simmering. I started and completed many other projects, including pitching and launching my brand new radio show, during the ensuing months while the book "stew" kept becoming richer and more flavorful by the moment. Bubbling away, preparing for its perfect time.

I had originally set my intention to finish the manuscript by the end of October. It was a somewhat arbitrary though logical date at the time I chose it. But as that date approached, I could feel in my heart that it wasn't time because the new revelations I was continuing to receive would expand the value and impact of the principles for the reader. Had I forced a late October birth, much of the detail, nuance, and richness of chapter 6, "Your Personal Board of Directors," would be absent because it didn't even exist in my consciousness yet. It would have been an okay book, but it would have fallen far short of what was possible. The resulting depth of the personal board aspect of my Discovery Framework, and the coaching experience that spawned it, earned me my moniker as "The Gremlin Coach." What a great example of the difference between fear-based procrastination and love-based percolation: the art of the productive pause. As always, it's the energy underneath our thoughts and actions—love vs. fear—that makes the difference.

I encourage you to apply these same guidelines as you read this book and begin making the principles a reality in your life. Easy does it. On the first reading, just let the concepts gently wash over and through you, leaving the first layer of residue for absorption. Letting any shift be as organic as possible is key to substantive, lasting transformation. Begin with one tiny baby step toward one small desired change. No amount of progress is too inconsequential to celebrate. Each step forward is an important opportunity to stop, consider what you've learned, examine your new tools, realize your new strengths, and embrace with gratitude the joy that will take you to the next step. Celebrating each success is key to fostering the constructive core energy that will keep moving you forward. Noticing and demonstrating love, respect, curiosity, compassion, and gratitude for any resistance to change is as important to moving forward as celebrating your successes.

Remember, whatever you have before you, if you can believe it and begin it, you can achieve it. In the words of singer/songwriter, Kathy Mattea, "Spread your wings, close your eyes, and always trust your cape!"

Thoughts on Organization Transformation

When I began to get clarity concerning the pervasive constructive impact of loving yourself unconditionally, a number of self-appointed advisors arose, warning that the falling-in-love-with-yourself paradigm might resonate with potential personal coaching clients but it would never fly with serious business professionals.

I'll admit, I took notice at first. My response was that I didn't care, that if all I ever accomplished was to help people transform their personal lives, I would have served a high calling in this lifetime. While that lofty-sounding answer was true, it had fear as its underpinning and therefore fell far short of my potential opportunity to foster real, extensive, lasting change on a global scale. The Universe let me go about my business until I was ready to get honest with myself about the fear, examine it with curiosity and respect, heal it with compassion, transform it with love, and accept the full scope of my calling with gratitude.

On that day, I remembered what I always knew in my heart: there is no substantive, sustainable organization transformation without individual personal transformation. I don't care how compelling the business case, comprehensive the systems, streamlined the processes, clear the roles, elegant the communication, comprehensive the training, or valuable the rewards. There is no meaningful, enduring organization transformation without personal transformation. This is equally true whether the organization is professional (a small business, government agency, or Fortune 500 company) or personal (a marriage, family, or friendship). Significant organization transformation always begins with each individual being fully committed to personal transformation.

All of the destructive and dysfunctional thoughts, feelings, and behaviors we humans exhibit in life personally and professionally have their roots in fear. Fear is the absence of love. If every one of us knew that we were Divinely Sourced and knew that we held limitless intrinsic power, worth, and resources, all of the backstabbing, territorial squabbling, and sabotage would end, along with the raping and pillaging of our environment, the scarcity-based greed, and the cheating, lying, and stealing.

When the energy we have invested in those destructive fear-based endeavors is freed up to be focused on constructive love-based endeavors, the shift will be phenomenal. When genuine self-love takes the place of fear-based self-obsession, what wonderful lives we will create for ourselves.

That's the type of organization transformation consultant and coach I am. One who helps individuals free themselves from self-imposed, fear-based limitations and harness the power of love so they can step into their greatness and, in constructive, cocreative collaboration with their fellow human beings, change the world.

I'm sometimes asked if, as a life coach, I coach business situations.

Yes, I coach *everything*, because *life* includes *everything*. I hold multiple professional coaching certifications, including board certification. I'm also retired from a thirty-year consulting career specializing in human resources and organization transformation, including serving as a senior partner in four of the world's largest and most prestigious global professional services firms. By virtue of my experience and expertise, I am well qualified to coach executives and professionals at all levels concerning a multitude of business situations.

Going beyond qualifications, the real answer is that life is just *life*. Despite our best efforts to separate our work and personal lives, those boundaries prove artificial, superficial, and highly permeable. Whether a client comes to me wanting help with a work situation or a personal relationship, inevitably, the lines blur. Wherever you go, there you are. How you do *anything* is how you do *everything*. When you fall in love with yourself, everything else falls into place, *personally and professionally*. Choosing love as your core energy changes your perceptions, opportunities, relationships, and priorities. You release the illusion of separation and embrace the truth of oneness. When love transforms your relationship with yourself, *it can't help but transform your personal life, your work, and the world.*

Gender-Specific Pronouns

Whatever pronoun I use, assume gender neutrality in all descriptions, especially those of the Divine and your personal board of directors. It makes much smoother reading to vary the use of masculine, feminine, and neutral pronouns than to constantly indicate female or male in every instance.

Great Expectations

This book includes real stories from my own life and the lives of my clients. The lessons are a treasure map to help you discover the unexplored possibilities buried within your authentic self. They provide a guide to turning those possibilities into realities that will restore you to wholeness. Every day, people just like you are moving forward into lives they love. By exploring their stories and the lessons they've learned, *you* can apply the same powerful insights to bring about the changes that will move *you* forward into the life *you* dream of.

Acknowledgments

Words cannot begin to express my eternal love and gratitude for everyone who has befriended and supported me on this journey, most especially the following people.

My Divine Source for the many gifts It bestowed on me:

- a vivid imagination
- the analytical abilities, creative vision, and perseverance with which to bring that dream to life
- a deep love of cats
- the gift of song
- my calling as a liberator, healer, teacher, and guide, to which It always holds me accountable

My personal board of directors, whose roles are explained in chapter 6—my sage Claire, my guardian Ella, and my muse Bee—for their unending wisdom and friendship. The insights in this book are Divine in origin, but every word was lived and written with them.

My treasured clients—past, present, and future—through whom I continue to learn so much about the ongoing Journey to Wholeness and the power of unconditional self-love. Though ethical commitments to privacy preclude me from naming them here, their names are forever inscribed on my heart and soul.

My beloved coaching cats—SiddhaLee, Mortimer, and Maisy Jane—for their fierce loyalty, constant companionship, profound feline insight, entertaining antics, and commitment to holding sacred space during the biggest personal growth spurt of my life. In particular,

- SiddhaLee, my resident feline sage, for his wisdom and hand-holding throughout the writing;
- Mortimer, my resident feline guardian, for maintaining household order, structure, and safety; and
- Maisy Jane, my resident feline muse for making sure I exercise my creativity, have fun, and avoid drudgery.

My husband, Wilson Ray Abney, for his love and loyalty, quirky sense of humor, belief in me, meal and movie breaks, unflagging enthusiasm for the written word, untold hours of brainstorming, and countless hours helping me refine my conceptual models and the language that describes them. I thank God he's such a left-brain word fetishist that he actually enjoyed it.

My son, Matthew Dungan Abney (aka Matt), for the lessons I learned through parenting him, for the laughter and silliness we've shared, and for the loving and responsible adult he has chosen to become. Just thinking of him always makes me smile.

My mom, Gladys "Gladdie" Elizabeth Aust Wells, for sharing with me her deep sense of spirituality, the joy of laughter, and her love of music, cooking, and reading. For being my biggest cheerleader throughout this project and reminding me that no matter how old you get, it's still a delight to know you are your mom's precious baby girl.

My dad, John Wesley Wells, Sr., for encouraging the engineer and artisan in me and for living his belief that *"girls can do anything."*

My nan, Grace Marion Adams Aust, for loving me to pieces and sharing with me her passion for fashion, flowers, and Cape May, New Jersey.

Barbara Kay Escher (www.yourmarketingteam.com) for her friendship, marketing insights, writing expertise, persistent push to begin blogging, and essential role in all aspects of birthing the original client success stories that were among the earliest seeds for this book. Through the ups and downs of our more than twenty-five-year relationship, I learned some of life's greatest lessons about the complexity of friendship, the importance of healthy boundaries, and the power of forgiveness.

Anne Elizabeth Barton (www.annebarton.coachesconsole.com), my loyal, patient virtual assistant who totally gets me and without whom everything would have gone twice as slowly and been half as much fun. I thank God every day for the great gift of our partnership.

Anne Marie Pettit, one of my first consulting bosses and my lifelong friend, for remembering all the good times and forgetting the days when I drove her crazy. For always making me so welcome in her family and life and for the July 2012 ten-day writing retreat in Villanova and the South Jersey Shore. The first pages of this book, as a book, I wrote at all hours of the day and night in my pajamas in one of her two homes. Her friendship and hospitality are precious gifts.

Louis "Barry" MacHale III, my dear pottery mentor, artistic coconspirator, and friend. I celebrate and honor his Spirit every day through the joy of creativity he helped me rekindle in my life so I could inspire it in others.

My core spiritual communities, including

- New Dawn Center for Spiritual Living in Aurora, Colorado (Rev. Karen Paschal, www.scienceofmind.org);
- The New Dawn Licensed Practitioners, who prayed me through the final weeks of drafting the manuscript for this book (Dave Peck, Eugene Holden, Sharon Jones, Mary Karuszas, Barb Pons, Clydene Smith, and Carol VanFleet-Swift);
- Prairie Unitarian Universalist Church in Parker, Colorado (Rev. Jann Halloran, www.prairieuu.org); and
- Unity of Littleton in Littleton, Colorado (Rev. Janet Lang, www.unitylittleton.org).

My personal fellowship of lightworkers (Jenni Prince, Deanna Kayyali, David Teich, Sandi Metzer, Sandi Ausman, Rebecca Blackbyrd, Jeanne Sanderson, and Patricia Keel) for all they did individually and collectively to expand my consciousness of what's possible and move me along my own journey as a lightworker.

My most excellent technology coaches, Jaan Goad (www.goadweb.com) and Denise Rivas (www.rivastechnologycoaching.com), who held my hand as we sped up sometimes-steep learning curves to keep my elaborate operations running smoothly.

A vast array of professionals from iPEC, the Institute for

Professional Excellence in Coaching (www.iPECcoaching.com), including

- associate director of training and my lead certification trainer, Janet O'Neil;
- vice president of marketing, Cindy Gardner; and
- my collaborator, client, and friend, vice president Liz Phillips Fisch, who invested considerable energy in reading this entire manuscript so that she could write a meaningful and authentic foreword.

Christine Kloser (www.transformationalauthor.com), the transformational catalyst, spiritual guide, and award-winning author through whose *2012 Transformational Author Experience* I received the knowledge and encouragement to share my message of hope and possibilities with the world through this book.

Everyone at Hay House/Balboa Press (www.balboapress.com) who helped publish and promote this book:

- Dwight O'Neal, who so wisely sold me on publishing with Balboa
- Eric Lundy, who convinced me to hire Balboa to promote the book globally
- Adriane Pontecorvo, who encouraged and managed me during the writing process
- Brandon Grew, who soothed and guided me through the meticulous editorial review
- Mary Hammon, the accomplished editor who refined and polished my message
- Andrea Geasey, who calmly led me through book layout and design
- Nicole Richardson, the gifted designer of my book's interior
- Alison Holen, the brilliant designer of my book's cover
- The countless others who contributed their talents to support the book's publishing and promotion

I am living proof: writing a book takes a village. I am forever grateful. You are loved and loving, blessed and a blessing. And so it is. Namaste.

Introduction:
Setting Sail

*When you fall in love with yourself,
everything else falls into place, personally
and professionally. When love transforms
your relationship with yourself, it transforms
your personal life, your work, and the world.*

O nce I began to experience the transformative power of
loving myself unconditionally, my constant wonder, joy, and
gratitude led to one conclusion: I must find a way to share
this great gift with the world. While I believe this book was conceived
the moment me taking human form this time around came under
discussion, it gained significant momentum at seven major turning
points during the past few years.

The first was enrolling in a life coaching certification program
offered by the Institute for Professional Excellence in Coaching
(iPEC) in September 2010. The second was launching my first
blog in October 2010. The third was beginning to write my clients'
stories of transformation in August 2011. The fourth was enrolling
in Christine Kloser's *2012 Transformational Author Experience* in
May 2012. The fifth was a combination writing retreat and vacation
in Philadelphia, Pennsylvania, and the South Jersey Shore in July
2012. The sixth was finding New Dawn Center for Spiritual Living
in Aurora, Colorado, in November 2012. The seventh was a three-
week writing retreat in January 2013, during which I completed the
manuscript.

The common denominator was a process of baby steps

through which I embraced and transformed fear so that I might step further into my calling to foster hope and personal transcendence through the power of unconditional self-love.

Turning Point 1

In 2009, one of my art students approached me about becoming her life coach. Honored by the request and a little freaked out by the possibility, I declined. Logically it made sense given my professional experience and expertise, but I still had much personal healing to do before I would be ready to coach others effectively.

By March 2010, out of overwhelming gratitude for being eighty pounds lighter physically, mentally, emotionally, and spiritually, all I wanted to do was find a way to share what I had learned and experienced with the world. I believed my story could help others find the lives of deep peace, lasting joy, and meaningful relationships they longed for. I had been similarly inspired in October 2008 when I read Elizabeth Gilbert's bestselling memoir *Eat, Pray, Love*. The author awakened in me the possibility that writing a book about my journey might encourage and inspire others with hope for what is possible.

My friend and marketing professional, Barbara Kay Escher, jumped on the bandwagon and began urging me to get my message of hope and possibilities out into the world. Yet despite a lifetime of journaling from the age of eight and a successful consulting career chock full of excellent writing, no one, including me, understood that I had become afraid to write. Or, more accurately, afraid to publish anything I had written. As a result, I continued to hide my light under a bushel a while longer.

On August 29, 2010, I told my husband that I didn't know how I was going to fulfill the deep calling I felt to help others, but it wouldn't involve taking tests or being judged by anyone. I woke up the next day feeling moved to Google life coaching certification programs on the Web. Smack dab at the top position of the ever-rotating list of sponsored Google sites was iPEC. Over the next two days, I researched their qualifications and approach, talked with their director of admissions, was accepted into the program, paid my admissions fee, and signed up for a nine-month life coaching certification program that makes boot camp look like a stroll in the park. Writing my first paper—a thirty-three-page review of my entire life—was sheer unadulterated *terror*. So much for no more testing or judging by third parties.

Turning Point 2

Ever the persistent midwife and undeterred by my increased coaching certification workload, Barbara continued pushing me to write my book. Using the *Julie and Julia* movie as evidence for how easy book writing can be, Barbara shifted her tactics to considering blogging as the path to publishing.

There was just one problem. I didn't do blogs. Didn't host them, contribute to them, read them—heck, I didn't even subscribe to any. At the time, I perceived bloggers as two types of people:

- self-absorbed egomaniacs who felt compelled to force themselves on the rest of the world or
- pitiful, shy people who only felt safe interacting with humankind anonymously.

I, of course, didn't want to see myself as a member of either group. In addition, I had two other problems with blogging:

- Some people write nasty, vile comments in response to blogs. I didn't want to help propagate any more intolerance and unkindness in the world. We already get plenty of that from political talk shows.
- I was busy and didn't have time to author or manage anything more than I was already handling.

Yet despite my brilliant arguments against me becoming a blogger, Barbara remained committed to getting me over the hurdle. One day, deeply enmeshed in the near-daily Barbara blog debate, she said, "I know you. Once you do it, you're gonna love it." Clueless as to the source of my resistance, we were both shocked when I responded by beginning to cry. Tears being a classic indicator that a big life lesson was lurking, I began to understand that this wasn't a mental block; it was a heart block. I centered myself, tapped into my tender, wounded heart, and began sobbing even more frantically, "I'm afraid. I'm afraid. I'm afraid." There, my friends, is the crux of the matter. There, my friends, is the crux of most of the pain and frustration we create for ourselves. The most offensive four-letter f-word I know: *fear.*

I wasn't afraid of helping people spew vile stuff at the Universe. I was afraid I would break again if they spewed it at me. Thanks to my son heading off to college and my husband's extended out-of-town job assignment, I had *become* one of those frightened people who was living alone and not interacting with humanity much. What life and Carole King had taught me to that point was that people were dangerous: "They'll hurt you. They'll desert you. They'll take your soul if you let them. So don't you let them."

Not one to give up easily, Barbara persisted by suggesting I start with a private by-invitation-only blog reserved for my nearest and dearest. Intrigued, I stopped crying. On the morning of October 9, 2010, thanks to Barbara's perseverance, my renewed courage, and the ease of setting up a blog site on WordPress, I awoke and published my first private blog post. Barbara was right; I did love it. So much so that I published my second post just two hours later, when I also took the site from private to public. That's me: in for a penny, in for a pound.

I refer to the first thirteen posts as the *Starter Blog.* Much like the tablespoon of starter culture that spawns a large new batch of homemade yogurt, those thirteen initial posts set in motion a process that would ultimately yield an outcome far grander than I could ever have imagined. I published no posts from mid-March 2011 until the end of June 2012, utterly consumed as I was by defining my signature life coaching approach, building my practice, serving my clients, and drafting this book. By June 30, 2012, once I was well into writing the book, I began blogging more succinctly and regularly. To subscribe to email notification of new weekly posts, visit tiny.cc/djwblog to sign up in the sidebar of my blog site.

You may access the thirteen original, highly sporadic blog posts that launched this book by visiting tiny.cc/djwstarterblog. The entries are in reverse chronological order. To read them in chronological order starting with the earliest entry, just begin at the bottom of the list and work your way up. These posts are living proof that writing from the heart with imperfect grammar can open the floodgates to serving the highest good.

Each of us has a personal story of transformation: our unique path from victim to victory, from breakdown to breakthrough. Every time you share your own story with others, you fan the flames of possibility in another's heart. You touch countless lives with hope through the ripple effect you set in motion when you share your story with each person you meet. How might *you* broaden the reach of *your* message today and every day? The world is longing to hear from you.

So what happened? The Universe loved me enough to keep pushing me outside my comfort zone. In a moment of grace, when I faced my fear, stopped resisting, and opened my broken heart to a new possibility, I fell in love again, this time with blogging. On that day, I knew how I would begin to write my book. I would do it in baby steps, one blog post at a time.

One of my favorite movies of all time is *What About Bob?* The film is about the transformative archetypal journey of the hero: the lesson that no matter how broken we are, with love and compassion, a dash of courage, a pound of commitment, and a sense of humor, we can do anything. We can learn and grow into happier, healthier people. Every one of us can find deep peace, lasting joy, and meaningful relationships. We do this through a lifetime of never-ending baby steps. Bless his heart, Bob baby steps his way all over the transformative Universe. Each time he pushes past his current limits to try something new, he is delighted. After his first sailing adventure (for which they had to tie him to the mast to get him to go along), he exclaimed to all he met, "I'm a sailor! I sail!"

On the day I published my first blog post, my world expanded yet again. I proclaimed to the Universe with every ounce of the Bob joy in me, "I'm a blogger! I blog!"

There's an old joke about a man in a flood who prays to God to save him. A rowboat passes by, but the man won't take it; he says he's waiting for God to save him. A speedboat, same response. Finally a helicopter, no dice. The man finally drowns. When he arrives at the pearly gates, he tells Saint Peter he wants an audience with God right away because he has a bone to pick with Him. Saint Peter obliges, and seconds later, the man stands before God. He rants, he raves, he accuses God of abandoning him: "I prayed for you to save me, and you did nothing. You call yourself God?" With gentle forbearance and a wry smile, God replies, "Fred, who do you think sent the rowboat, the speedboat, and the helicopter?"

We ask for the things we claim to want in our lives, and then we fight them because we're frightened by the new responsibility or because they don't arrive in the precise form we had in mind. Blogging was my "rowboat" to writing this book, touching more lives, and loving every minute of it.

Turning Point 3

Many coaches use brief testimonials that say things like, "This coach rocks!" As Barbara and I began talking with my clients about their experiences, we found their stories were more than testimonials. They were messages of inspiration—lessons in hope, courage, and triumph. Deeply personal opportunities to share the unique lessons each individual had learned about the life transformation that is possible when you learn to love yourself unconditionally.

We were certain one of the best ways to foster hope and demonstrate the possibilities for transformation in the lives of others was to allow my clients' results to speak for themselves by sharing their stories on my website. Barbara and I collaborated with them to write their stories, basing each on a different life lesson. I began publishing the earliest versions of these Lessons in Living under the "success stories" tab of my website in early 2012, including my own story, "The Lesson of Hope."

As more and more clients shared their stories, in spring 2012, I saw an opportunity to provide even greater value by creating a series of interactive self-study workbooks based on the lessons inherent in their stories. With the ongoing impact and evolution of the lessons; continued personal and professional experience, study, and growth; substantive blog posts; and a robust social media presence, my own unique life coaching perspective and voice began to emerge. By summer 2012, it became clear that pulling everything together into a book was one of the best ways to share my message even more broadly. I set my intention, and you now hold the result in your hand.

Many thanks to Barbara and the clients who graciously

invested their time in sharing with you so candidly from their experiences. While the stories are real, I have changed the names out of respect for privacy. Respecting that boundary is an important aspect of my code of ethics.

Turning Point 4

By May 2012, the stars and planets were in full alignment for me to move into the final stage of birthing my book. I had transformed my body, mind, heart, and soul, found my calling, become certified as a life coach and Reiki master, and thanks to my blog, client success stories, and website, I had tons of content with which to seed the manuscript. I just needed a little additional nudge to start integrating everything into a book. The Universe responded with an unsolicited email (one I actually read) that pushed me across the threshold into Christine Kloser's book writing program, the *2012 Transformational Author Experience (TAE)*.

Through Christine's program, in a two-week period, I participated in twenty-six one-hour educational teleseminars led by experts in all aspects of writing and publishing, including futurist Barbara Marx Hubbard (*Birth 2012 and Beyond*), author Neale Donald Walsh (*Conversations with God*), literary agent Bill Gladstone, New World Library Publisher/President Marc Allen, and Hay House/Balboa Press President/CEO Reid Tracy. At times, it felt like drinking from a fire hose; thank God I took notes and purchased unlimited rights to replay recordings of the sessions into perpetuity. By the time we were finished, I had been exposed to every angle, aspect, consideration, and nuance of writing and publishing my first book.

As an added incentive to get serious and get moving, the program provided the opportunity to submit a proposal for my transformational book by July 31, 2012 to be entered into a contest offering amazing prizes such as agency representation by Bill Gladstone, a print publishing contract with New World Library, and assisted-publishing contracts with Hay House/Balboa Press. Knowing from firsthand experience the valuable role a coach can play in helping us manifest our deepest longings, I happily purchased the platinum level option to join Christine, a renowned spiritual guide and award-winning author in her own right, for six months of group coaching to help me sustain my commitment and momentum. If you are serious about writing a transformational book—one that, as Christine teaches, will transform your life, your readers, your business, and the world—enroll in one of Christine's programs.

Turning Point 5

One of the bonuses offered with the platinum level group coaching upgrade to Christine's transformational author program was a mid-July 2012 three-day seminar in my birthplace of Philadelphia, Pennsylvania. The first day was a private networking session with Christine and twenty-five other platinum participants. It was an opportunity to discuss our books, receive coaching, and encourage each other forward on our individual paths to publishing. The second and third days involved joining a few hundred participants for a two-day immersion with renowned marketing and PR guru Steve Harrison on the ins and outs of publicity.

I wrestled with whether to purchase the platinum option. The cost was $697 plus travel, meals, and lodging. Well worth the price but still a substantial sum. I could minimize additional out-of-pocket expenses by covering the airfare and hotel with credit card points.

While I was weighing the pros and cons of participating, my dear friend and former colleague Anne Marie Pettit (aka Anna) suggested I arrive ten days early to enjoy an extended visit with her family and other former consulting colleagues from the Philly area. With the July 31 book proposal deadline just weeks away, a Philadelphia getaway would offer me the opportunity to focus on writing during the day and restore my soul by socializing with old friends in the evening. It was very tempting. When Anna sweetened the offer to include whisking me away for a weekend in my idea of paradise (the South Jersey Shore), I enrolled in the platinum program happily.

As we so often do, after making my decision, I continued to wrestle a bit with whether I had invested my assets wisely. Every time the doubt surfaced, I would stop, breathe, close my eyes, recenter, assess the energy underneath my decision (love) and the energy underneath my doubt (fear), clear myself, recommit, and keep moving forward.

In the months leading up to the Philly trip, the Universe sent two additional confirmations that I had made the optimal decision. The first came in the form of a two-hundred-dollar rebate on the enrollment fee when I won a drawing on one of the group coaching calls. Ta-da! The second was a call from my son and his fiancé, letting me know they would be joining me for the weekend at the South Jersey Shore, including a return visit to the Wildwood boardwalk.

The trip was heavenly. I spent a week with Anna and Jim at their home in Villanova, Pennsylvania. There I found myself nestled among the many landmarks of my childhood and early career:

- two miles from Bryn Mawr Hospital, where I was born
- fifteen miles from Media, where I grew up
- four miles from St. Davids, where I attended college at Eastern University
- eighteen miles from Centre City Philadelphia, where I spent the first seventeen years of my consulting career
- one hundred miles from Cape May, New Jersey, where I spent many idyllic days with my beloved nan in her tiny home on Maryland Avenue, just two blocks from the beach

The combination of a change of scenery, writing isolation by day, and reconnection with lifelong friends at night provided the perfect fuel to help my words flow forth effortlessly. Many evenings, after returning from a night of fun with friends, energized and inspired, I would begin writing again at Anna's dining room table until the wee hours of the following morning. At which time I would go to sleep for six to eight hours, wake naturally, and begin again.

As the writing/reveling/writing/sleeping pattern continued at the Shore, I not only made substantial progress on the book proposal but also conceptualized, completed, and scheduled twenty additional blog posts I would release over the next ten weeks. My proposal was quickly becoming a book, and having launched a new weekly blog campaign in mid-June (*Declare Your Independence from Stress*), I was firmly established in blogging one or more times a week. There was no longer any question: I am an author! I publish!

In the company of my friends, I had the opportunity to visit nan's grave and marvel at the miraculous expansion and rehabilitation a couple from Princeton, New Jersey, had wrought with nan's itty-bitty bungalow. My friends and I delighted in the easy camaraderie of lifelong companions who enjoy an unbreakable bond. We have certainly had our share of disagreements through the years. Some originated in my tendency to become bossy and driven under pressure. Others in Anna's habit of throwing whipped cream at me during seventeen consecutive company Christmas parties (which, it just occurred to me, may have been her antidote to my propensity for intensity). Nevertheless, our connection runs so clear and deep that we never stay angry with or abandon each other. We always find a way to forgive and forget any relationship missteps and make our way back to the playful and supportive intimacy we treasure.

So what was the significance of this particular turning point? With publication of a book looming, my visibility and vulnerability would be raised considerably. I might be criticized, rejected, or worst of all, ignored. Still stinging from recent censure by a friend, without knowing it, through my trip to Philadelphia and the South Jersey Shore, I had chosen the perfect remedy to any fear of rejection. I fed my sense of belonging by reconnecting with my roots. I reminded myself of this profound truth: no matter what fear-based lies and illusions I may be choosing to believe at any given time, we are all always essentially one. Whether my book sells two million or two hundred copies, is a commercial success or only an important milestone on my personal journey, I am known and loved by myself, my Divine Source, my family, my friends, and my Philly tribe.

Turning Point 6

During my own personal Journey to Wholeness, I discovered, one at a time, the four inner senses and their roles in fostering the life of flow I sought (chapter 5). By late fall 2012, feeding my inner senses of creativity, vitality, and spirituality was a firmly established way of life—a healthy new habit. My sense of belonging still required more attention. With the dramatic changes in my interests and values, some of my existing relationships had become even stronger. Others had begun to dissolve naturally. Participation in my two existing spiritual communities (Prairie Unitarian Universalist Church in Parker, Colorado, and Unity of Littleton in Littleton, Colorado) continued to provide substantial support to my personal Journey to Wholeness. After many months of introspection, renewal, and growth, I found myself seeking additional alliances that would resonate to my new core beliefs, provide opportunities for me to be of service, and support me in my lifelong journey to even greater wholeness. In the idiom of the day, I needed to find more "peeps."

In early November 2012, I was blessed with the discovery of an additional spiritual community: New Dawn Center for Spiritual Living in Aurora, Colorado. From the first visit, I knew I had found a source of fulfilling personal relationships and a spiritual home. A group of people with whom I could share my gifts and who would help fill my desire for companionship and continued mutual growth.

The pace and ease of my writing took huge leaps forward when New Dawn licensed practitioners began supporting me weekly with affirmative prayer. Without their friendship and encouragement, I might have finished this book eventually, but it wouldn't have been nearly as smooth, quick, or comprehensive. I am forever grateful. The day I found New Dawn was indeed a new dawn in the birthing of this book.

Turning Point 7

When I began summarizing how this book came into being, I thought there were just three turning points. Over time, as my journey continued evolving, the Universe added three more. Then, in the final weeks of completing this manuscript, the Universe offered me the seventh and final turning point in the form of a three-week writing retreat in my Aurora, Colorado, home.

In early January, good friends were moving from Virginia to Texas. They asked if my husband, Wilson, and I could join them for the first week to help them unpack and settle in. With the launch of my radio show that week, there was no way I could be away from home without Internet access. Having retired a year earlier, my husband was free as a bird. We compensated for me not participating by having him help them for *three* weeks.

Originally, I'd planned to complete my book manuscript by

the end of October 2012. When new revelation started coming fast and furious in October, it was clear the Universe had a different idea about the breadth and depth of the book. I revised my target date to December 30. By mid-December, when I realized that only force, not flow, was going to produce the book by New Year's, I switched my perspective to, "It will be done when it's done," letting go of all preconceived notions about timing. I'd learned from experience that force is based in fear. Fear-based energy produces less-than-optimal results that rarely last, while sucking the joy out of the process. This book would be fueled by love. The Universe was in charge of letting me know when it was finished. My job was to stay tuned to the Universal frequency and keep taking dictation.

In preparation for my husband's departure to Texas on January 14, we talked about the potential benefits of having no other humans in the house. (The cats get very upset if I refer to it as living alone; with the three of them engaged in every aspect of my life, including coaching clients, I *never* live alone.) Still, there were occasions when I referred to the trip as Wilson "abandoning me when I was coming down the home stretch on finishing my first book." A few times, I even found myself moved to tears when I thought about it. What was going on? I was the one who had suggested extending his trip from two weeks to three. Where was this abandonment energy coming from?

Knowing that tears always signal an opportunity for new growth, I set my intention to receive the insight. I sat alone with my eyes closed and asked, "What form of misery are you remembering or creating for yourself with fear-based thinking, little one?" The answer came immediately. I had confused Wilson's departure this time for his departure four years earlier, when he left for a three-month out-of-town job assignment that had stretched to three years. When he left that time, I was burned out, eighty pounds heavier, and ten years into a severe bout of depression. Although his taking the job had been a joint decision, I felt abandoned and petrified. Nonetheless, it became the portal to the greatest transformation of my entire life. A success story in every possible way. My psyche was totally forgetting the *facts* and channeling the residue of leftover fear-based abandonment energy it had found in some ancient dark corner. As I cleared the fear-based lies and illusions and embraced the love-based truth and reality of my transcendence, I stepped back into the light.

The day Wilson left, the writing began pouring from me at an astonishing rate. No force, just flow. Every time I'd think I was finished for the day, I'd receive more insights, run to the laptop to "make a couple of notes," and find myself completing a new chapter an hour or two later. I continued to eat well, exercise daily, and get even more rest than had been my norm over the previous year. One night I slept for eleven hours straight with vivid dreams in which I resolved a variety of current life dilemmas and got insights into the next chapters of the book.

So what had happened? Wilson was never an impediment to my writing. He was supportive, respectful, and minimally disruptive. His heading out of town for three weeks was an opportunity to remember that I experienced the greatest transformation of my life during the three years I lived without humans in my house because it focused my energy like a laser on what needed attention in my own life. This "retreat" would be equally momentous; this time I would finish writing my first book.

Over the preceding seven and a half years, the Universe had taken me on an incredible journey from burnout and despair to hope and transcendence, to independence and wisdom, to service and community. Whether I live with or without humans, cats, or other species, I am never alone. My Divine Source dwells within me. When I remain free of fear and centered in love, I experience the Divine in every being, encounter, and circumstance. When I stay tuned to the Universal frequency, I constantly receive new insights and suggestions about where to go and what to do. As a conduit for Divine love and light, I have endless opportunities to partner with others looking for a guide on their Journeys to Wholeness. Whatever my circumstances, I know *who* I am and *Whose* I am: a unique cocreative expression of the Divine.

It is so fitting that I delivered the manuscript for this book to my publisher on Valentine's Day 2013. Writing it has been a labor of love. I am honored to have been entrusted by the Universe to share my message of hope and possibilities with the world. And I am grateful that I had the courage, resources, and support to do so.

Part I: What's Love Got to Do with It?

One of the problems with not taking care of our health is that the effects of ignoring it are often slow to show up. We continue to juggle family responsibilities, work, and finances until we lose ourselves, waking up one day fifty pounds heavier in body and soul—no good to ourselves or anyone else.

There is hope for getting off the wheel and living a life you love. It all starts with embracing the amazing and liberating possibility that the love of your life just might be you.

Approaching myself and my life—every being, encounter, and experience—with love, respect, curiosity, and compassion always reveals and advances the highest good.

Maintaining a belief in abundance and an attitude of gratitude anchors each moment in a sense of generous, effortless, gracious flow—a life of freedom centered in being, not doing.

Chapter 1:
The Lesson of Hope

If despite a lifetime of diligence and hard work, you feel you are still searching for something that remains just beyond your grasp, then you, my friend, may be stuck in the hamster wheel approach to life. Hamster wheel people don't give up; they will die trying to deliver the goods.

You may think you want a better job, more satisfying relationship, or healthier body. In reality, your restlessness isn't about your income, your relationships, or your looks. It's about feeling incomplete.

As a life coach and Reiki master, I am in the business of liberation. I help people escape the self-imposed prison of the hamster wheel. For many years, their stories were my story, and they may be your story as well, but they don't have to be. There is hope for getting off the wheel and living a life you love. It all starts with embracing the amazing and liberating possibility that the love of your life just might be *you.*

If you are like many others, you may doubt that falling in love with yourself is even *possible* let alone *powerful*. I assure you, *it is*. To help you begin to accept that you too have the power to embrace this reality, I will share with you the short version of my own personal story of transformation. The story of what happened in my own life when I finally fell in love with myself.

Mine is an all too common tale. Too many years on the wheel resulted in utter exhaustion and despair. I was the classic successful Type A overachiever. Sensible, driven, hardworking, and financially secure. Someone you could *always* count on to get the job done.

I began life in 1954 with a question mark over my head. Back then, medicine could not assure the survival of an "Rh factor" baby.

Some required many blood transfusions. I was one of the fortunate few who needed just one.

Instead of perceiving my survival as a blessing and a gift, early on I concluded that I had to pack each day with output because I was, after all, operating on borrowed time and someone else's blood. My response to a gift of grace was a lifelong marathon of trying to *prove* myself worthy through productivity.

Prove myself I did! Along the way, I earned a full scholarship to college and graduated *summa cum laude* in three years. Sounds great but at what price? Anorexic, ulcer ridden, and clinically depressed by age nineteen, I thought I had to re-earn my right to be here every day. To be worthy and safe, I had to control every aspect of my life, always pushing, always moving, always working, always doing. Looking back, I now realize that when I chose the following couplet from Sara Teasdale's poem "Dust" (1966) as the caption for my college yearbook picture, even at age twenty-one I already knew somewhere deep in my soul that this way of living was a very slippery slope. Sara writes,

I almost gave my life long ago for a thing
That has gone to dust now, stinging my eyes—
It is strange how often a heart must be broken
Before the years can make it wise.

Although I was usually a quick learner, it would require three more decades of experience before I was finally compelled to act on that inner wisdom. Meanwhile, the world kept right on rewarding my perfectionism and incessant productivity. Fresh out of college, I got a job in management consulting, making partner in my first firm at age thirty. Over the next thirty years, I served as a senior partner in four of the world's largest and most prestigious global professional services firms.

I had some wonderful times in that career. I traveled all over the world, mentored young people, and knew the satisfaction of doing good work. But even the most committed and productive individuals can shift from frustration to a sense of futility when their values, passion, work, and lives become disconnected. After decades of working nonstop with little attention to my personal health and welfare, my soul and my role had become increasingly separated, leaving me feeling disillusioned and betrayed by the very life I'd created.

One of the problems with not taking care of our health is that the effects of ignoring it are often slow to show up. We continue to juggle family responsibilities, work, and finances until we lose ourselves, waking up one day fifty pounds heavier in body and soul—no good to ourselves or anyone else. It's no surprise that during the final years of my consulting career, morbid obesity and profound depression defeated me daily. This led me to conclude that my only hope of escaping the rat race that was *slowly* killing me was to get it over with *once and for all*. The great irony was that while I started out feeling afraid I'd die if I didn't keep working all the time, I ended up knowing I would eventually kill myself if I couldn't find another way to make the pain stop.

Yet as *unbelievable* as it may sound, today, in my late fifties, I find myself in the best health of my entire life. While I still have ups and downs, my days are permeated with deep peace, lasting joy, and meaningful relationships. These great blessings are the result of a Journey to Wholeness that began in 2005 when I retired from consulting. At that time, I was neither fit nor motivated to start another career. Though I completed a couple of graduate courses with the intention of starting my own organization consulting firm, I found myself too burned out to pursue it seriously.

For the first time in my life, I had no clear plan for my future, just the knowledge that I would have to find a way to heal my self-esteem and restore my mental and physical health even to *have* a future. In autumn 2006, when my son left for college, my husband and I moved from Virginia to Colorado, believing a dramatic change of scenery might provide a nurturing climate for my healing.

Inspired by Julia Cameron's book *The Artist's Way* and still a consultant at heart, I embarked upon a path of self-healing involving rediscovering the artistic joys of my youth while facilitating groups around artistic recovery and discovery. In the process, I began teaching art privately on a small scale. Though I loved my work, the expenses of my small business substantially exceeded my income. Morbid obesity and profound depression persisted. In a five-week period during the spring of 2008, my cat, my father, and my beloved pottery mentor died, adding the challenge of overwhelming grief to my daily mix.

Meanwhile, my husband had been trying to find work locally. After two years with no luck, we jumped at the chance for him to take a *temporary* ninety-day job back in Washington, DC, making money doing work he loved. The ninety-day assignment stretched to three years, with weeklong visits home every three to six months.

I remember the day his car pulled out of our drive as if it were yesterday. While I was supportive of our decision, I was both excited and anxious about living alone for the first time in my life. I had always assumed the role of perfectionist caretaker and confidante, first in my family of origin and then again in every relationship, job, and household. Who was I if there was no one else for me to take care of? The Universe definitely has a sense of humor. There I was, living alone at the age of fifty-five with responsibility for the only person in my life that I'd never taken care of—myself.

I spent the first four months hating being alone and bemoaning all the things I didn't like about my life. Then one day, in a rare moment of clarity, I received a Divine download: "You can spend the next year making yourself miserable over all the things you can't control, or you can see this as an opportunity. Is there anything that's completely within your control and, if you achieved it in the next year, would plant joy firmly in your soul no matter what your other circumstances might be?" My response? "I have got to lose this weight." The most incredible journey of my life began in that simple moment of grace.

My Journey to Wholeness started with regaining a sense of control over my physical care—what I ate and how I exercised. Losing eighty pounds—and keeping it off—is the part of the story that many people respect and even envy. But that was just the tip of the iceberg. If all I accomplished were to change my body through healthy eating and exercise, I would have stopped far short of the wholeness I was seeking.

I had my next life-transforming realization forty pounds into my eighty-pound weight loss—high on healthy fuel, cardio-induced beta-endorphins, and the thrill of, once again, being able to do something I set my mind to. While a healthy diet and significant daily exercise were necessary factors, they were only the price of admission to attaining the life of deep peace, lasting joy, and meaningful relationships I desired.

Once I understood that excess physical weight is often just a symbol for excess spiritual weight, I realized finding wholeness is not primarily about losing body fat. It involves caring enough about myself to create an environment in which I nurture and cherish all aspects of myself.

With this realization, the Universe tapped me on the shoulder once again: "The key to living a life you love is to feed all of your senses in a balanced way, so no one sense will take over, trying to fill voids it can never hope to fill." I got the broader insight into this download another twenty pounds later. Sensory balance doesn't just apply to the five outer senses through which we celebrate our external world but *also* to the four inner senses of creativity, vitality, spirituality, and belonging, through which we imbue our experience with meaning.

As one who suffered anorexia at age nineteen and obesity at age fifty, I believe both have their roots in an unhealthy relationship with food—trying to use food to fill un-food needs. For me, both were ways of coping with anxiety—misguided attempts to feel safe by creating the *illusion* of control over a life spinning madly *out of control.*

The major reason many of us can't sustain the positive results of diet and exercise is that most programs do not get to the root issue—an imbalance in the care and feeding of our souls. I learned to pay attention to how I am feeding all of my senses—content and frequency—and whether each is being starved, smothered, or healthily sustained. While my weight loss certainly involved more mindful and nutritious eating as well as regular exercise, the degree of success and ability to sustain a healthier, happier, more harmonious lifestyle was much more dependent on balanced feeding of *all* nine senses.

Through daily self-reflection and written meditation, I started to recognize and adjust my sensory imbalances. In the process, I realized that the most important element in manifesting the life of my dreams was a stronger bond between my Source and myself. Through the power of *that* synergy, I found more-meaningful relationships with everyone and everything.

Prolonged isolation gave me the opportunity to work on the relationship I had neglected my entire life—the relationship with myself. Stripped of my habitual pattern of avoiding my own needs and feelings by focusing on caring for others, I finally understood that loving and taking care of myself is one of the greatest gifts I can ever give myself or anyone else, because when I nurture and cherish myself, my *very presence* encourages and supports others. When I'm *not* taking care of myself, I'm not able to give my best to anyone or anything. I may put on a good show, but it will be a pale imitation of the real thing.

Where did these insights take me? Over a period of two years, I shifted from taking good *care* of myself to falling in *love* with myself. When I fell in *love* with myself, everything else in my life finally fell into place. The transformation was so profound, I could literally feel my soul and role reuniting in a new form. No longer a hamster trapped on a wheel but a vibrant, joyful, fully engaged woman. I said good-bye to obesity, along with a ten-year bout of debilitating chronic depression, and said hello to life!

At this point in my story, you may well ask, "What would falling in love with myself look like?" Remember the last time you fell in love with someone else? How did you treat the object of your affection? You probably thought about him a lot, paid attention to his needs, and treated him as if he mattered. Because, to you, that person did matter; he mattered a great deal. In fact, you probably became downright obsessed with every aspect of your beloved.

Falling in love with yourself looks just like that: paying attention and treating yourself as if you matter. Because you do; you matter a great deal. You are a unique cocreative expression of the Divine. *You* are the only *you* we've got. *You* are a precious natural resource not to be taken for granted.

As I lived my new commitment to loving myself, I discovered that my sense of equanimity and fulfillment were greatest when I fueled my core energy in constructive and loving ways—physically, mentally, emotionally, and spiritually. But as I worked more deeply with the concept of love, I found the term to be nebulous, tricky, and easy to misunderstand. With experience, I was able to increase the clarity of my intention to love myself by adding the attributes of respect, curiosity, compassion, and gratitude. I discovered the following:

- Approaching myself and my life—every being, encounter, and experience—with love, respect, curiosity, and compassion always reveals and advances the highest good. Moment by moment, I know where, how, and when to invest my energy to move myself forward on my Journey to Wholeness.
- Maintaining a belief in abundance and an attitude of gratitude anchors each moment in a sense of generous, effortless, gracious flow—a life of freedom centered in *being*, not doing.
- Most surprising, important, and delightful of all, when I fall in love with myself again and again, everything else in my life really does just fall into place.

The result? I discovered my purpose gradually by committing myself to unwavering self-awareness grounded in cherishing myself *unconditionally.* As I did so, I came to understand that despite balance sheet evidence to the contrary, I hadn't *failed* at making a living *with* my art. I had instead received a much more precious gift. I had saved a life, my own, *through* my art. By creating a life worth living, I had learned the art of living—enjoying the journey. My own life *is* my greatest creative work.

The journey that began with transforming my own life shifted naturally into meaningful work as a life coach and Reiki master, through which I help others discover that health, peace, and joy are possible for them as well. If it's possible for me, it's possible for anyone. If any of us is worthy of such a life, we all are.

I close this chapter of my story where I began: mine is a story of hope; yours can be too. Fall in love with yourself and live the life you dream of. You are worth the effort.

For more insights into everyday approaches to loving yourself, read *The Art of Extreme Self-Care* by Cheryl Richardson.

Chapter 2:
The Lesson of the
Oxygen Mask

Flight attendants instruct us on every flight that should an oxygen mask drop down in front of us, we *must* put on our own masks before attempting to help anyone else. That seems selfish and counterintuitive for most of us. First we want to help our child, parent, spouse, or frightened seatmate. It can be difficult to accept the fact that we will not be able to help anyone else if we run out of oxygen ourselves.

We might be more likely to accept the truth if the flight attendants painted a picture of what *could* happen if we *don't* put on our own masks first. Imagine a scenario in which you are traveling on a plane that develops engine trouble. Suddenly, oxygen masks drop down and your seatmate just stares at his, frozen with panic while precious seconds tick by.

If you choose to ignore the flight attendant's instructions and struggle to get a mask on a panicked person first—in a plane that may well be unstable—you may wait just a bit too long to take care of your own mask. At that point, you are no good to yourself or anyone else.

Suppose instead that you recognize the common sense in the flight attendant's instructions. You decide it's not just okay but *essential* to take care of yourself first and only then assist your fellow traveler. Once you have your seatmate settled, you glance across the aisle and notice someone else frozen with panic. You reach across, help them, and then motion for them to help the next person over. Eventually you find that you have helped someone who helped someone who ... You get the idea. When the flight stabilizes and you land safely, you know with every fiber of your being that you have been anything but selfish.

Unfortunately, we rarely notice how well the "oxygen mask" principle applies to everyday life, but does it ever! The parallel is that failure to take care of your own health will inevitably mean you will be unable to care for the ones you love. Though the damage can be slow in showing up, one day you wake up weighed down by a load you can no longer bear—physically, mentally, emotionally, or spiritually.

What if you used the oxygen mask as a symbol of *self-awareness* in your daily life? Sitting right in front of your face at all times. Put it on, breathe deeply, and new choices appear. Not selfish choices but honest ones that allow you to set priorities that nurture you and those around you on a Journey to Wholeness.

Remember what it felt like to be able to help others on the airplane because you first took care of yourself? As you become increasingly self-aware and able to make constructive choices, you become a positive example for someone else, who becomes a positive example for someone else, and so on. Like the ripples in a pond, your new self-awareness requires no pushing or directing to move outward and touch others. It just happens.

My client Lisa feels that the most important changes she has made in her life through coaching with me are self-awareness, living with intention, and having compassion for herself. She has also lost thirty pounds, but in her words, the weight loss is "just the outer indication of significant inner change."

"When I was introduced to Deborah, I had been putting in thirteen- and fourteen-hour days establishing myself in a new profession while caring for my dying mother. I was overweight, with my body and spirit stretched to the limit. That seemed normal because, for me, hard work has always been both a joy and a legacy."

Lisa's mother was raised in a small coal-mining town where they grew their own food or they didn't eat. Recreation as we know it today didn't exist.

Growing up as the oldest of ten children, Lisa's mother shined in her daughter's eyes as the greatest role model any girl could have. Her mother's young life consisted of washing the clothes and working in the company store. Over the years, Lisa watched her mom always do the right thing. She was the person Lisa wanted to be.

"Unlike my mother, I was blessed with greater bounty. My parents worked all the time, and we would never have gone hungry. But my brother and I worked side by side with my parents and were fulfilled by knowing that our work could help support the family too. Looking back, it shouldn't surprise me that my parents' legacy of unending hard work became the bedrock of my life as well.

"Over time, I became a life coach, committed to helping others integrate the physical, mental, emotional, and spiritual aspects of their lives. I quickly discovered that even coaches need coaches."

In our first session, Lisa told me she wanted to lose weight. Little did she know that physical weight loss would be the smallest part of what she gained from our work together—a byproduct rather than an end in itself.

"The larger lesson was becoming sufficiently self-aware and detached to see that I needed to start by having greater compassion for myself. Deborah helped me realize how the negative energy of my relentless inner taskmistress was weighing me down and holding me back from the joy-filled life of service I desired.

"Many people tell us that we should take care of ourselves, but how can I manage to have compassion for myself when my beloved mother is dying? How can I do what I need to do for my mother and still embrace the hurting self who can't imagine who she will be without her mother?"

Only when Lisa could detach and begin to see herself from the outside was she able to embrace the grieving part of herself who was eating for comfort. None of her past diets had taught her that. Until she began to get it, meaningful, lasting change was unlikely. By serving as a loving mirror—listening deeply, trusting my intuition, and asking penetrating questions—I was able to help Lisa get past the distraction of her external body weight to see the root of her unhappiness: the unbearable weight her heart and soul were carrying on the inside.

"Today I eat and live with greater intention. I've lost thirty pounds. There is vitality and light in my life even as I rework my priorities and commitments to ensure that my mother's final days are as peaceful and as filled with love and comfort as I can make them.

"To demonstrate real compassion for others, I had to first put on my own 'oxygen mask' and have some compassion for myself."

For more insights into the role of self-compassion, read *Start Where You Are* by Pema Chödrön.

Part II:
The Discovery Framework

The Discovery Framework helps us clear ourselves of fear-based limiting beliefs and discouraging self-talk so we may tap into our deepest wisdom and move forward in each moment with confidence, peace, and joy, living lives of flow.

Establishing and maintaining constructive core energy fueled by love, respect, curiosity, compassion, and gratitude forms the firm foundation for a life of flow.

That fuel allows you to realign your awareness with what I call the "God's-eye view," enhancing your perception and expanding your perspective until you know that we are one and that Universal love is always unfolding the highest good for all, in all, through all.

When we feed our outer and inner senses in a balanced way, they build on our energetic foundation, like the framing in a home, to provide the day-to-day infrastructure for a life of flow securely grounded in constructive core energy.

When the members of your personal board of directors collaborate respectfully, they leverage their vast collection of competencies, seamlessly drawing on your constructive core energy and feeding all of your senses in a balanced way.

The tools for fostering flow are a set of simple personalized practices that help you realize the essential shift from believing these principles in your head to living them from your heart.

Chapter 3:
Setting Your Intention—
Living in Flow

As I sit down to write this section of the book, I am a little intimidated by the prospect. While the book has been many months in the making, in general, the writing has flowed smoothly with little anxiety. The sections have unfolded organically, either from existing writing or as new insights were revealed. Why is this one proving a greater challenge?

Birthing the Framework

The major components of the Discovery Framework started being revealed to me during my own recovery and transformation a couple of years ago. Further details are revealed to me each day as I live it and coach it. While my intellect has been involved in creating diagrams and charts to illustrate the constructs, most of the time my head stays out of the game. This is consistent with my intuitive "dancing in the moment" approach to coaching.

I start and end each day with meditation to clear myself of all fear, open myself wide as a clear channel for love and light, and set my intention to dedicate my thoughts, words, and deeds to supporting the highest good for all, in all, through all. I reconfirm that intention before each coaching session. My intuition, home of my deepest wisdom and strongest connection to my Divine Source, takes the lead, speaking through me to my clients. While that flow is augmented periodically with reasoned structural input from my intellect and the application of discernment (the blending of intuition and reason), the process is most effective when I keep my head out of the lead position as much as possible.

I listen deeply, apply discernment, and recognize the main elements of the framework in action, along with new aspects being revealed by each individual's unique persona and experience. The framework is neither linear nor static.

Therein lies the challenge for sharing it in print. Because books, by their very nature, *are* linear and set in stone, or type as the case may be, we expect them to unfold section by section in an orderly, sequential fashion. While this makes achieving clarity concerning the framework more complicated and slower going in print rather than when coaching in the moment, I appreciate that I can support the journeys of more people more quickly and affordably through the written medium.

As if this wasn't hard enough, the Universe decided now would be a good time to deliver the next set of life lessons I specifically requested a few months ago concerning setting healthier boundaries for my life. It upped the ante through a series of personal bumps in the road, which provided opportunities to walk the talk, deepen my own ability to live the framework, clarify my boundaries, and strengthen my commitment to my calling. The opportunities included two of my beloved cats being diagnosed with illnesses; my husband undergoing two surgeries in one month, with two more to come; and a rift in a long-term relationship.

Despite the complexity of the task itself and the additional lessons I learned from the relationship bumps in the road, as you can see, I did indeed write the framework chapters. They are sufficiently robust to start you on your journey but by no means exhaustive. It would be neither possible nor productive to contain every aspect of the framework in this one book. The elements and their subcomponents are so rich in interpretation and impact, each could spawn its own book, if not multiple volumes. Sharing all of it with you on your first exposure would be confusing, frustrating, and impossible.

The only way for these concepts to become a transformative reality in your life is for you to live them personally. Only you can determine the specific interpretive nuance that will optimize their impact in your life. You can only do that by living them moment by moment, day by day. The experience is not one of lining up discreet elements in a linear process. Living the framework is a unique, dynamic, interdependent, iterative, and evolutionary journey. While you *may* find it complex at times, you will *always* find it highly rewarding.

As I look around me, I see the Universe consistently demonstrating boundless creativity in every single aspect of its unfolding. Not just one of anything but a rich assortment of all. Countless animals, vegetables, and minerals. Myriad butterflies, flowers, and trees. Innumerable people, cats, and dogs. Many paths to wholeness.

This book shares the path that I discovered on my own Journey to Wholeness. I am here to be the unique Deborah Jane Wells cocreative expression of the Divine in this Universe at this moment in time. My role is to share my personal experience with others to make my contribution to revealing and advancing the highest good for all, in all, through all. This book is about hope, about believing a life of wholeness is available to each of us, believing that it is possible to find *your* path to it once you release the weight of *your* past disappointments and future fears. Whether my message inspires you to discover a path similar to mine or one that appears very different, I will have realized my intention: to inspire you to hope, dream, and act.

Framework Overview

What is flow, and what does falling in love with yourself have to do with finding it? When you fuel all aspects of yourself with love, respect, curiosity, compassion, and gratitude, you begin living in flow. Your life becomes a fluid Journey to Wholeness grounded in who you are *being*, not what you are doing. Every breath, thought, word, and act—your very presence—fosters a generous, effortless, gracious life of flow filled with faith, hope, prosperity, peace, and joy.

- **Faith:** I am confident that love is the greatest power in the Universe.
- **Hope:** Universal love is always unfolding the highest good for all, in all, through all.

- **Prosperity:** My Universal Source is excellent, limitless, and reliable.
- **Peace:** I relax into all that was, is, and will be.
- **Joy:** Whatever my circumstances, I know *who* I am and *Whose* I am: a unique cocreative expression of the Divine.

When living in flow, work, rest, and play all feel the same. Organic. Effortless. Force is not needed to accomplish anything; in fact, its use would be detrimental because force disrespects your deepest wisdom and greatest gift: your intuition. Rainer Maria Rilke said it this way, "May what I do flow from me like a river, no forcing and no holding back, the way it is with children."

One day, while neck deep in my first iPEC life coaching certification assignment—a thirty-three-page review of my entire life—I had a thought: What if all of my striving to make things happen was actually working against me? What if I was missing many of my best synchronistic opportunities because I was too busy working *my* plan, one I had cast in concrete? How might my experience be transformed if I just stayed more centered in the present moment, clear in *who* I am and *Whose* I am, not trying to architect my life down to the last detail? Here's how the Universe replied:

- That day's daily word reading from Unity was entitled "Synchronicity."
- My daily reading from Julia Cameron was on synchronicity.
- My Pema Chödrön and Wayne Muller daily readings were also on synchronicity.
- The daily creativity prayer from Julia Cameron was on synchronicity.
- The Dr. Wayne W. Dyer audio lecture I finished that day closed by extolling the virtues of trusting in synchronicity. Align yourself with Source Energy and the Universe will support your endeavors.

Just me, just here, just now, just be. Does that sound lovely but unrealistic and maybe just a bit "out there?" Living in flow is not only desirable; it's possible. In the remaining chapters in this section of the book, I will share with you the keys to living a life of flow through my core coaching model—the Discovery Framework. I started developing the framework during my own transformative journey. As I began to feel substantive, constructive, lasting changes in my own life, I became curious about what was happening.

I knew that paying attention was key to sustaining my new way of living. Ever the coach, my greatest desire was to be able to capture what I was experiencing to help others find more joy-filled lives. As I explored, documented, and analyzed my experiences and those of my clients, the Discovery Framework (figure 1) began to take shape. It has continued to expand and evolve daily during the past two years. Its content and impact will continue to broaden and deepen as our lives continue to unfold.

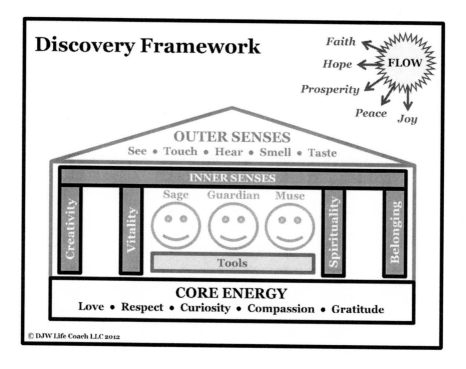

Figure 1: Discovery Framework

Having introduced you to the first element of the framework, flow, here is a brief roadmap of the remaining elements:

- **Choosing Your Fuel—The Role of Core Energy.** Establishing and maintaining constructive core energy fueled by love, respect, curiosity, compassion, and gratitude forms the firm foundation for a life of flow.

- **Creating Balance—Feeding Your Nine Senses.** Like the framing in a home, our outer and inner senses build on our energetic foundation to provide the day-to-day infrastructure for a life of flow securely grounded in constructive core energy. Sensory balance involves feeding all of our senses in healthy, balanced ways so that no one sense takes over trying to fill voids it can never hope to fill. This begins with mindfully feeding our five outer senses, through which we celebrate our world, and it extends to intentionally feeding our four inner senses of creativity, vitality, spirituality, and belonging, through which we imbue our experience with meaning.

- **Achieving Equanimity—Your Personal Board of Directors.** You may say, "So far, the principles sound great in theory, but you've neglected to take into account the oppressive power of the judgmental voice in my head. Every time I start to break free from thoughts of self-imposed limitation and lack, that voice puts me back in my place by reminding me that I'm not good enough and never will be." Good news! Help is on the way. Once you build a more constructive relationship with your personal board of directors—sage, guardian, and muse—you will find that disparaging voice becomes less prevalent *and* less powerful. When your board members collaborate respectfully, they leverage their vast collection of competencies, seamlessly drawing on your constructive core energy and feeding all of your senses in a balanced way. When fueled by love, your board members are capable of synthesizing their diverse strengths and talents into a whole that is much greater than the sum of its parts.

- **Making It Happen—Tools for Fostering Flow.** If you are like many, at this point you are wondering, "The framework is elegant and intriguing but a bit complex. In practice, how do I work with my board of directors to apply the principles consistently enough to turn this way of living into a healthy new habit?" That's precisely where my tools for fostering flow come into play. This set of simple personalized practices helps you realize the essential shift from *believing* these principles in your *head* to *living* them from your *heart*. Making these tools a way of life helps you stay centered in flow. When you drift off center occasionally, as any of us can do when overwhelmed by stress and gripped by ancient self-destructive scripts, these tools are the key to recognizing it quickly and getting back on track easily.

Your ability to experience flow in any moment, filling your life with faith, hope, prosperity, peace, and joy, is directly proportional to your ability to fuel yourself in that moment with love, respect, curiosity, compassion, and gratitude. That fuel allows you to realign your awareness with what I call the *God's-eye view*, enhancing your perception and expanding your perspective until you know that we are one and that Universal love is always unfolding the highest good for all, in all, through all.

I know it sounds complicated. Please breathe and relax into it. Breathing is always a good idea and one of the tools for fostering flow.

Flow Scan

Now that you have greater understanding of the attributes of flow, I know you will want to begin experiencing it. Whenever you have the sense that you are stuck or blocked, a real-time flow scan can help you identify which aspects of your thinking would benefit from recalibration and what form that might take.

Flow Scan

I approach life with love, respect, curiosity, and compassion, revealing and advancing the highest good.
My gratitude for Universal abundance anchors each moment
in generous, effortless, gracious flow filled with faith, hope, prosperity, peace, and joy.

	FEAR-Based Lies and Illusions Blocking Me		FLOW	Baby Steps to LOVE-Based Truth and Reality
DISTRUST		FAITH	I am confident that love is the greatest power in the Universe.	
DESPAIR		HOPE	Universal love is always unfolding the highest good for all, in all, through all.	
SCARCITY		PROSPERITY	My Universal Source is excellent, limitless and reliable.	
PANIC		PEACE	I relax into all that was, is, and will be.	
MISERY		JOY	Whatever my circumstances, I know who I Am and Whose I Am.	

© DJW Life Coach LLC 2012

Figure 2: Flow Scan

Figure 2 provides a simple form to guide this process. The scan consists of a five-step process, with each step grounded in caring enough about yourself to do the following:

- Pay attention so that you notice quickly whenever you are feeling stuck.
- Invest your energy in assessing the fear-based lies and illusions that are blocking you, identifying any feelings of distrust, despair, scarcity, panic, or misery.
- Determine what baby steps will restore your life to a love-based truth and reality of faith, hope, prosperity, peace, and joy.
- Hold yourself accountable for following through on your commitment to take action.
- Assess your results and continuously refine and expand your action plan to fill your reality with the truth of love-based flow and minimize succumbing to the lies and illusions of fear-based blocks.

You're worth the effort. With practice, you will become adept at noticing whenever you're feeling stuck or blocked and quickly taking action to restore flow. This way of living will become a healthy new habit through which you will begin building the less stressful, more fulfilling life you dream of.

The remainder of this book will provide more details and examples from my clients. Flow life lessons infused with stories of transformation and transcendence from real people just like you— responsible, capable, hardworking, well-intentioned. People with unfulfilled hopes and dreams. Trapped by fear and the mistaken belief that busyness was the same as purpose, my clients couldn't stand the way they were living but felt powerless to change.

In *making* a living, they forgot to make a life they actually *enjoyed* living. One that resulted in them springing out of bed each morning with eager anticipation for the as-yet undiscovered potential that would be unveiled throughout that day. One that included falling asleep easily and peacefully each night, filled with gratitude for all they had experienced and the opportunity to rest and recharge for another exciting opportunity-filled day tomorrow.

Living the Discovery Framework is a process of baby steps. Slow and steady produces meaningful, lasting results. Vast, forced output is rarely sustained. Great strides of lasting value involve myriad baby steps over time.

Fortunately, time is not a scarce resource. That's right: time is *not* scarce. We have all the time we need for the things that matter. Our sole responsibility in each moment is to discern, using intuition and reason, what matters most right now, to focus, and to follow through. Remembering this great truth is another tool for fostering flow. According to noted psychologist, Abraham Maslow, "If our true nature is permitted to guide our life, we grow healthy, fruitful, and happy ... [Yet] ninety-eight percent of us die before we taste the nectar of our magnificence."

The remaining chapters of this section introduce the other elements of the Discovery Framework. I will illustrate the concepts with selected examples of how they have manifested in my life and in the lives of my clients. The purpose is to provide you with some tangible ideas from which you can begin your personal exploration of the optimal ways to implement the principles in your own life.

Inspired by the words of Leo Tolstoy, Dr. Wayne W. Dyer urges us, "Don't die with your music still inside you. Listen to your intuitive inner voice and find what passion stirs your soul. Listen to that inner voice, and don't get to the end of your life and say, 'What if my whole life has been wrong?'" The Discovery Framework has helped many clear themselves of fear-based limiting beliefs and discouraging self-talk so that they may tap into their deepest wisdom and move forward in each moment with confidence, peace, and joy, living lives of flow. If you will relax into the concepts and open your body, mind, heart, and soul with faith and hope to the possibility of a new way of being, I know the framework can be a powerful force in your life as well.

For more insights into finding flow by being fully present in unconditional self-love, read *A Life of Being, Having, and Doing Enough* by Wayne Muller.

Chapter 4:
Choosing Your Fuel—
The Role of Core Energy

Establishing and maintaining constructive core energy fueled by love, respect, curiosity, compassion, and gratitude forms the firm foundation for a life of flow.

- **Love:** I nurture and encourage myself in healthy ways.
- **Respect:** I honor my choices; I do the best I can with the love and light I have at the time.
- **Curiosity:** Instead of judging, I wonder why.
- **Compassion:** I acknowledge and value my feelings.
- **Gratitude:** I appreciate my life; everything is an opportunity.

Approaching life with love, respect, curiosity, and compassion always reveals and advances the highest good for all, in all, through all. Gratitude fosters a life of generous, effortless, gracious flow filled with faith, hope, prosperity, peace, and joy (figure 3).

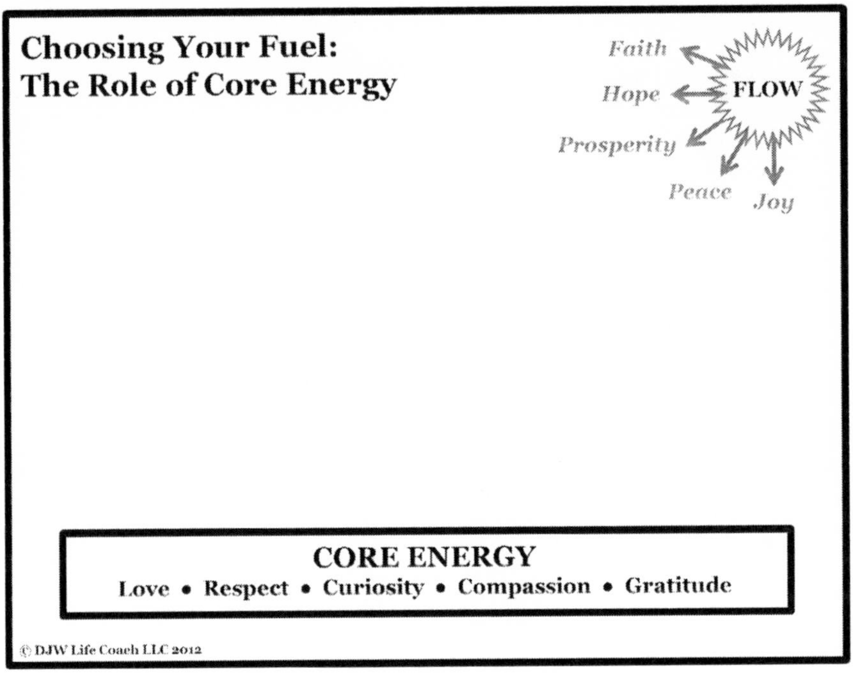

Figure 3: Core Energy

It all starts with embracing the amazing and liberating possibility that the love of your life just might be *you*. Many people tell me it feels selfish to think in those terms and that we are supposed to love and care for "our neighbor." I remind them we are also supposed to "love our neighbor as ourselves." Many of us would end up in court or prison if we treated our neighbors the way we treat ourselves.

I am reminded of the adage, "Charity begins at home." If, according to Merriam-Webster's 2011 dictionary, charity is "benevolent goodwill toward or love of humanity" or at a minimum "lenient judgment of others," then I suggest it *has to* begin at home; it *has to* begin with me. My ability to love others unconditionally is directly dependent on whether I love myself unconditionally. While, as a good actor, I can fake it by keeping all the judgmental voices inside my head, as with many things in life, there is a vast difference between faking it and the real thing.

So what does this kind of love look like? According to a well-known treatise on the subject found in 1 Corinthians 13:4–8 of the Bible (New International Version),

Love is patient, love is kind. It does not envy, it does not boast, it is not proud. It does not dishonor others, it is not self-seeking, it is not easily angered, it keeps no record of wrongs. Love does not delight in evil but rejoices with the truth. It always protects, always trusts, always hopes, always perseveres. Love never fails.

Imagine applying these to yourself. Being patient with and kind to yourself. Not being envious, believing you deserve the best of everything. Always honoring and trusting your personal truth. Respecting your abilities and the decisions you have made. Always nurturing and protecting yourself. Persevering with loyalty to yourself no matter what. Paying attention to and demonstrating compassion for whatever you are feeling. Recognizing and being grateful for your many gifts and talents. Pierre Tielhard de Chardin captured the importance of this way of living when he wrote, "Someday, after mastering the winds, the waves, the tides and gravity, we shall harness for God the energies of love, and then, for a second time in the history of the world, [we] will have discovered fire."

This is the very heart of the personal transformation I've experienced in my own life and the lives of my clients. With the compassionate guidance of the spiritual elders listed in the appendix and many more, I am learning to harness the energy of love and approach myself, every being, encounter, and experience with love.

This way of living is a path, a journey, not a destination. It is not about self-improvement. It is about becoming aware and awakening my heart, moment by moment, day by day. This path to deep peace, lasting joy, and meaningful relationships begins with a three-part commitment to myself:

1. I matter.
2. I fuel myself with optimal constructive energy.
3. I am powerful.

It is interesting that those who learn to fall in love with themselves are actually less likely to behave selfishly. Their joy and peace are contagious. They show up in their families, friendships, and workplaces with a spring in their step and a zest for living that carries them, and those around them, forward in new and exciting directions.

My clients are men and women; young and not so young; single, divorced, or married. What they have in common is an unflinching commitment to knowing themselves better and doing the deep and rewarding work necessary to make the lives they dream of a reality.

Their real-life stories and mine send a clear, consistent message: when we spend our lives not taking care of ourselves, eventually we are no good to ourselves or anyone else. We cannot share anything of lasting value with others by giving from an empty well. When we learn to treat ourselves with love in every moment, then—and only then—will we find ourselves able to be of genuine service to others.

My clients inspire me every day with the certainty that all of us can make this Journey to Wholeness. If you are ready to take life-changing action, then you have been led to a place where you will find the answers you seek. As my clients learn to love themselves unconditionally, they are transforming their lives. You can too.

The bottom line? It's not just *okay* to fall in love with yourself. It's *essential*. When you fall in love with yourself, everything else finally falls into place. This transformation arises from a fundamental shift in your head and heart. Once love transforms your relationship with yourself, it can't help but transform your personal life and work in ways that will exhilarate you. Your more constructive personal energy will automatically transform every being and situation you encounter. You will, by your very presence, quite literally transform the world. The Discovery Framework provides a useful model for making this way of being a reality in your life too.

Love, respect, curiosity, compassion, and gratitude are not just five woo-woo, New Age words I pulled out of thin air because they sounded Zen and cool. They were revealed to me individually, real-time as I lived through the phases of my own dramatic and highly personal transformation. The formula for making them a way of life is simple to explain. In every situation, love yourself enough to pay attention to every aspect of your life. Respect everything you are experiencing—what you are thinking, feeling, deciding, saying, and doing. Determine whether the energy underneath is love or fear. If it's love, you are probably on your authentic path. If it's fear, demonstrate compassion for yourself. Foster gratitude by reminding yourself that everything is an opportunity. Then further neutralize the fear by bringing curiosity to bear. Explore every aspect of the situation, especially your internal landscape, and identify all of the opportunities available to you through this unique experience. As with any new skill, practice will help this way of being become a healthy new habit—your automatic response to every situation.

In summary, figure out what you want, understand whether it's fueled by fear, transform any fear into love, set your intention, and then get ready to receive it, because it *will* happen.

In the remaining sections of this chapter, I'll provide an overview of the five elements of core energy. While a few words of explanation will help you get started, the only way to understand how to optimize their constructive impact in your life is to live them. Begin by setting your intention to make them a way of life. Once your energy is fully committed, *the Universe will deliver*, often quite rapidly. After all, with his famous e=mc² formula, Albert Einstein proved that everything is energy. Quantum physics demonstrates that energy attracts like energy. So, having selected and tuned yourself to the desired frequency, your personal versions of love, respect, curiosity, compassion, and gratitude will be manifested in your life. You will discover the many ways they show up for you and what approaches to applying them are optimal to create the life *you* dream of. With practice and experience, they will become your new norm.

Love

I nurture and encourage myself in healthy ways.

My first big realization on the road to recovery was that my utter and complete burnout was clear evidence that I had not been loving myself. I was not nurturing or encouraging myself in healthy ways physically, mentally, emotionally, or spiritually. I was disrespecting my body, mind, feelings, and values. Working myself nearly to death with no regard for illness or despair. If I had treated another being that way, human or feline, I would have been jailed long ago.

When I became serious about uncovering the roots of my imbalance and trying to set it right, I concluded that there are two fundamental types of core energy: love and fear. When I examined the primary energy underneath any thought, feeling, word, or deed, I found love, fear, or some combination of the two.

Love is constructive and moves you forward. Fear is destructive and holds you back. Love is the author of truth and reality. Fear is the author of lies and illusion. At first, I didn't always recognize them as love or fear because they didn't always show up in my life with those specific labels. I found the terms to be nebulous, tricky, and easy to misunderstand. With awareness, persistence, and unflinching honesty, over time I was able to recognize love and fear masquerading under lots of other masks.

In trying to get a more concrete grasp on what healthy self-love might look like, I realized I understood its opposite, fear, much better because I had fueled myself with it for so long. With mindfulness and curiosity, I recognized that the many faces of fear could be synthesized into a four-part pattern that captured the most common guises in which fear showed up in my relationship with myself—contempt, judging, shame, and lack (figure 4). I then employed one of my favorite writing technologies, the Microsoft Word thesaurus function, to find their opposites—respect, curiosity, compassion, and gratitude. With the help of the insight and clarity provided by those particular attributes of love, the light dawned, and I began to make real progress. Focusing on these four constructs helped me more easily answer the eternal question in every situation: "Is this what unconditional self-love looks like, and if not, what would bring me closer to that intention?" I will expand on the nature and meaning of respect, curiosity, compassion, and gratitude in the remaining sections of this chapter.

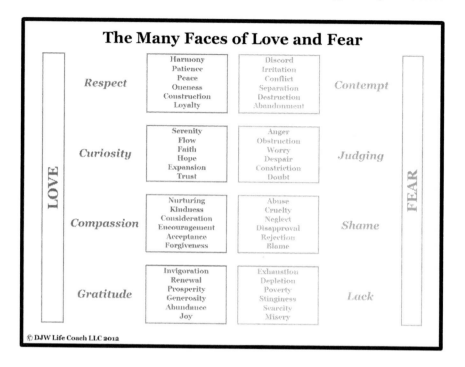

The Many Faces of Love and Fear

		LOVE		FEAR	
Respect	Harmony Patience Peace Oneness Construction Loyalty	Discord Irritation Conflict Separation Destruction Abandonment	*Contempt*
Curiosity	Serenity Flow Faith Hope Expansion Trust	Anger Obstruction Worry Despair Constriction Doubt	*Judging*
Compassion	Nurturing Kindness Consideration Encouragement Acceptance Forgiveness	Abuse Cruelty Neglect Disapproval Rejection Blame	*Shame*
Gratitude	Invigoration Renewal Prosperity Generosity Abundance Joy	Exhaustion Depletion Poverty Stinginess Scarcity Misery	*Lack*

© DJW Life Coach LLC 2012

Figure 4: Love and Fear

Throughout this book, I will sometimes explore one of the four attributes of love in particular. At other times, to be more inclusive, for simplicity's sake I will just use the term *love* with the intention that you read into it the other four attributes as well. It will make for smoother reading if I don't repeat all five words every time I intend to invoke them.

While taking good care of myself physically produced many healthy changes, when I shifted from taking good care of myself to falling in love with myself, everything else in my life finally fell into place. I lost weight physically, mentally, emotionally, and spiritually. I got off the hamster wheel, found my calling, and created a joyous, fulfilling life. Falling in love with myself was just like falling in love with someone else. I paid attention and treated myself as if I mattered, as if I were my own beloved child.

One of the most powerful changes was being relentless about noticing and transforming any negative head talk into more loving, supportive messages. In chapter 6 on your personal board of directors, we will dive much more deeply into the roots, role, and transformation of this type of self-sabotaging gremlin head chatter. For now, just know that fear is incredibly toxic; it doesn't take much to poison the well of your life. Little things like the verbs I use—*have to, should, need to, can't,* and the like—are indicators that fear is fueling my thoughts and beliefs about a given situation or relationship. Nothing is too small to matter; every little bit of fear you transform into love gives you a substantial energetic boost. It doesn't take much fear to bring you down. Letting go of even a little will raise you up.

Months after I began writing and teaching about the love-fear energetic dichotomy, I started encountering it all over the place. The message is shared by many of the world's great spiritual teachers. Though surely I must have encountered this lesson before, I had either misunderstood its application or experienced a common barrier. Head knowledge hadn't been enough to make a difference. I needed to learn it for myself from painful personal experience. I needed to take life's longest journey: the eighteen inches from my head to my heart.

Having made the journey to unconditional love for myself, it is no surprise that when I went looking for a professional coach training school more than a year later, I chose iPEC with its core philosophy of Energy Leadership: learning to lead your own energy so it works for rather than against you. In his *Energy Leadership* book (2008), iPEC founder Bruce D. Schneider refers to the two core energies as anabolic and catabolic. To paraphrase his description, anabolic energy is healing and growth-oriented. It helps you achieve beneficial results and is useful in leading others to do the same. In contrast, catabolic energy is draining and potentially toxic to you, your organization, and everyone around you. Clearly, Bruce and I were swimming in the same pond. Here's my credit card. Sign me up!

Through the iPEC Certified Professional Coach (CPC) and Energy Leadership Index Master Practitioner (ELI-MP) certifications, I acquired specialized knowledge, tools, and skills. I incorporated these into my signature approach, along with my Discovery Framework, to strengthen and deepen my ability to help my clients assess and transform their personal energy from fear to love in every situation.

Respect

I honor my choices; I do the best I can with the love and light I have at the time.

Unconditional self-respect begins with mindfulness—caring enough about myself and my experience to pay attention to what is happening and what I am feeling. If I don't recognize when I'm feeling stressed, I can't do anything to change it.

Respect is also about not beating myself up for past choices— things I thought, said, did, or didn't do. It's about knowing that I am doing the best I can with the love and light I have access to at the time. Every experience is an opportunity. As I am able to recognize and transform more of my fear-based limiting beliefs into love-based empowering truths, I gain access to greater wisdom, clarity, and confidence, moving myself further along my personal Journey to Wholeness. By learning to demonstrate unconditional respect for myself in every moment, I become more able to demonstrate it for others as well.

Respect is also about boundaries, being clear where mine end and yours begin. Many of us find it hard to set clear and healthy limits on what we will and won't allow others to do to us. Even more of us have difficulty not violating others' boundaries.

Consider this example from my own life. On Monday night, my spouse comes home from work miserable about how his boss is treating him. It pains me to see my husband so unhappy. I listen patiently and sympathetically to sixty minutes of complaining. I tell him exactly what he needs to do. He doesn't do it. Tuesday night, he comes home singing the second verse of the boss abuse song. I listen *less* patiently and repeat, with additional rationale, what I told him to do the night before. He shuts down and retreats to his den to watch football. Wednesday night, same song, third verse. This time I don't listen *at all*, blow a gasket, and tell him to stop being a wimp. He demonstrates just how much of a wimp he isn't by getting royally annoyed with me and storming off to the den. I demonstrate just how much of a wimp I am not by following him into the den and repeating my suggestion with even greater volume and specificity, including what he can do with the horse he rode in on. The good news—my husband's boss is now completely off the hook because we are now so angry at each other that what his boss is doing to him pales in comparison.

Some of you are taking my side: She's a professional management consultant and life coach with more than thirty years' experience. What moron wouldn't immediately implement anything she suggests? Others are taking my husband's side: She's a pushy overbearing know-it-all who's taken three months to write the final three chapters of her book. Why doesn't she stop sapping his self-confidence and mind her own business? To both sides I say, "Blah, blah, blah."

The root of the problem is not whether my suggestions were wise. The issue is the nature of the core energy underneath me providing suggestions in the first place. Input stemming from a supposed "desire to help" becomes interference when it is fueled by fear in the form of anxiety, self-doubt, avoidance, or arrogance. *Anxiety* is when I can't stand whatever pain I am choosing to feel over the choices he is making, and in order to stop my pain, I need to get him to choose a different path. *Self-doubt* is when I fear that if he isn't making the same choices for his life that I'm making for mine, maybe I'm wrong. *Avoidance* is when there are aspects of myself I'm not yet willing to address, so I distract myself by focusing my need for personal growth on him instead. *Arrogance* is when I dare to presume that I can run his life better than he can, despite the fact that I've not walked even one mile in his shoes. The common denominator in each case is that fear, not love, is the core energy fueling my suggestions.

In the scenario of my husband's problem with his boss, my real goal wasn't to help my husband. My goal was to relieve my own fear-based pain at experiencing his pain. My goal was to stop his pain as quickly as possible so that I could stop my own. What I was doing didn't "come from a good place"; it came from fear. From wanting to fix it for him to release myself from fear faster instead of respecting him enough to fix it himself when the time was optimal for *his* highest good. The tip-off was that I got annoyed when he didn't take my suggestion—annoyance being one of fear's many ugly cousins. It is nothing short of arrogant of me to think I could possibly run my husband's life better than he could.

I'm asked all the time if this means it's always wrong to make suggestions or try to teach anyone anything. No, that is not what it means. Here's how to tell the difference between making a respectful suggestion and disrespectful interference. When I am coming from respect, I have no energetic charge over whether you act on what I share. When I'm being respectful, I'm fully and creatively engaged in the process with no attachment to the outcome. Disrespect is evidenced when I get hooked by what you decide to do or not do: either relief or happiness when you do it my way or anxiety, frustration, or anger when you don't. Either reaction demonstrates that I am a little too invested in how you live your life. When I feel neutral about whether you do or don't adopt my suggestions or act on the information I shared, I'm coming from respect.

This lesson was driven home for me dramatically when I heard the following story a couple years ago. In late fall, a man stood enthralled watching a caterpillar spin a cocoon on a branch outside the kitchen window. All winter long, the man watched over the cocoon, amazed at how it withstood the onslaught of freezing rain, blizzards, and harsh winds. When spring finally arrived, the man was relieved to see the cocoon still hanging in there. As spring ripened into summer, the day finally came when the butterfly began to make its departure from the cocoon. The man watched the butterfly work to break free. The process went slowly and looked difficult. The man became impatient with how long it was taking and anxious that the butterfly was suffering. He could hardly bear to watch. Finally, beside himself with frustration and worry, the man decided to help. He took a small pair of nail scissors and carefully cut the cocoon open wider to allow the butterfly to escape more quickly and easily. Alas, the butterfly did escape but died just a few minutes later. What appeared to the man as a needless struggle was actually crucial developmental time the butterfly needed to be able to thrive outside the cocoon. Robbed of that added growth opportunity, the butterfly never developed the strength it needed to survive and flourish.

When I first heard this story, I sat at my kitchen counter and sobbed; I finally got it. All those times when, energized by my own fear, I had interfered with another's life, I had been decidedly unloving. When I disrespected the other's personal path by trying to shortcut her opportunity to learn in her own way and time, I had demonstrated anxiety, self-doubt, avoidance, and arrogance.

While the lesson of the chrysalis didn't result in me ending all fear-based interference overnight, it has made me much more aware of what's energizing my actions. In those situations where fear and a lack of respect are my fuel, I am faster at detaching and releasing myself and the other person to walk our authentic individual paths with love and light.

These examples don't just demonstrate the subtlety of respecting others' boundaries; they point the way to respecting my own. Without a doubt, the greatest violator of my own personal boundaries is me. I am the perpetrator of unconscionably disrespectful words and acts against myself. Much of it happens in the confines of my own head.

When I use my thoughts to undermine my self-confidence and punish myself repeatedly for past "mistakes," I am abusing myself. When I incessantly rehash painful scenarios from my past, I cause myself far greater injury through that repetitive instant replay than the original abuser ever caused me. When I communicate to myself in subtle and not-so-subtle ways that I don't matter, am not good enough, and am powerless, I am being cruel. When I tell myself I'm crazy to keep thinking, saying, and doing the things I do, I disrespect my journey and myself. Most of us never say anything half as loathsome to others, even in our most enraged moments, as we say to ourselves daily in casual conversation. Respecting ourselves means zero tolerance for self-judging and self-abuse.

Curiosity, the next aspect of love we will explore together, will prove a great aid in escaping the many destructive patterns of disrespecting ourselves and others.

Curiosity
Instead of judging, I wonder why.

Fear festers in dark and isolation. The moment you expose fear to examination in the light, you begin to dissipate its power. Nowhere is this more true than when fear shows up as its relentless ugly cousin, judging.

When I talk about judging or judgment, I'm not referring to

having good or bad discernment. I'm talking about judging yourself, other people, and situations in dualistic terms such as *good* or *bad*, *right* or *wrong*, *okay* or *not okay*. When we judge things by such simplistic, restrictive polarities, we limit our options, get stuck, and block ourselves from the highest good. When we can neutralize the judge, we get unstuck, expand our possibilities, and increase our ability to grow and move forward.

One of the great miracles in life is how even a small change in your perception can dramatically expand your perspective. When a ship at sea changes course by just one degree, one hundred miles later it is in completely different waters than it would have been without that small modification in direction. Internal shifts are even more profound. It is downright miraculous how even a small change in your perception can dramatically expand your perspective.

As human beings, many of us have a robust judging dialogue running in our heads much of the time: *This is good for me. That would be bad for you. I was bad to do that. You were good to do that. You were bad to say no. I was good to say yes.*

We're not talking about torturing ourselves over real danger or life-and-death situations here. We're talking about how much you spent on that blouse. Why you ate that second piece of pie at dinner. Why you tend to become impatient with your youngest child. Why you keep gaining weight. Why, no matter how hard you try, your mother-in-law can find the flaw in anything you do. Why despite his promise to do so, your husband never remembers to put the trash out on Wednesday nights. Judging is a prison of our own making.

We obsess until we've turned something inconsequential into a huge, paralyzing, misery-making melodrama. The solution is quite simple: just say no. Next time your brother-in-law or the voice in your head wants to play the blame game with you, *just say no!* Demonstrate greater creativity and suggest a game of curiosity instead.

Start with a question like this: *If I am mistaken about his motivation, what might really be going on? If this isn't about me, what are three other potential explanations that have nothing to do with me? And if one of those is the real explanation, what role do I choose to play in this situation?*

Because whether it's the voice in your head or the one coming from your older sister, you don't have to play any role. You can listen politely and say, "I appreciate you sharing that. Let me ponder it and get back to you." Then go about your business. You do not have to engage in every potential disagreement you're invited to. Newsflash: in *your* life, *you* are the great decider.

Once you get the knack, you're going to love the feeling of trading judging for curiosity. It's not a forced march, a different set of rules you must follow to be a "better" person. It's a gift of grace accepted freely and with gratitude, an honor and a privilege filled with joy and wonder. By discovering possibilities you never imagined, you open the door wide and go bounding through to endless opportunities.

Sometimes, despite copious curiosity, there is no clear, 100-percent-verifiable answer. In those situations, Dr. Wayne W. Dyer taught me to ask, "Which thought moves me forward?" For example, I can't prove or disprove to a 100 percent certainty the presence of an all-loving, all-knowing, all-powerful Life Force in which everything is sourced and empowered. I find believing in such a Force expands my opportunities and moves me forward in loving, wise, powerful ways, whereas believing life is random and meaningless leaves me depressed and stuck. For me, it's an easy choice: I choose being fully alive.

Given that judging is a prison of our own making, here is an added bonus, your so-called get-out-of-jail-free card: 95 percent of the time, other people do things for their own reasons. It has nothing to do with me. Even when it looks like it's directed at me, even when they tell me it's all my fault, there's a 95-percent chance it still has little or nothing to do with me. The corollary is also true: even when I think it's all *your* fault, most likely it's not. It's probably mostly about me. We each carry around so many assumptions, filters and lenses from our culture, families, past disappointments, and future fears that it's nearly impossible for any one of us to be the sole cause of anything in someone else's life.

So if it's not about me, instead of making myself crazy with destructive head chatter, how about investing my energy in being curious about what it might really be about. Better yet, how about releasing you with love, light, and respect to figure that out for yourself? Meanwhile, I can choose to do the same. Focus my energy on *my* own life, learn *my* next lesson, figure out what *my* next opportunity might be, and keep moving *myself* forward on *my* own path. Because, as we learned in the section on respect, I'm here to be the best *me* I can be. What you choose to make of your own life is completely up to you.

Becoming conscious and claiming your personal power to neutralize the judge will yield immeasurable benefits. You will literally be able to redefine your world, because there is no absolute reality, only the story you tell yourself about what is happening and what it means. Every being, encounter, and experience that comes my way is filtered through a conglomeration of lenses that results in my unique perceptions. These lenses cause me to see my world in a certain way. They are influenced by my unique and complex mix of myriad factors: the family, cultural, and societal norms I was taught; my physical and mental abilities; my personality and natural talents; my birth order; the patterns I deduced from all my past experiences; and the assumptions I've presumed concerning what's likely and possible in the future. I create my reality in each moment by choosing what I will think, believe, feel, and do based on what my lenses allow. I can choose to look through the lens of fear and remain weighed down and self-imprisoned, or I can choose the lens of love and embrace a life of freedom and flow. No outside event or situation, no other person can dictate my attitude.

However unconscious the process may feel at the time, I am manifesting the world I *choose* to see. This is the reason the game of golf can be perceived as *any* or *all* of the following, depending on your lenses:

- a delightful afternoon immersed in nature
- an exhilarating and rewarding competitive event
- a fun way to exercise with friends
- an endless day of humiliation and torture

Let's look at my own experience with golf to access this insight more deeply. When we lived on the East Coast, my husband and I owned a vacation home in the Blue Ridge Mountains. When my son, Matt, was eleven years old, we enrolled him in kids' camp to help him enjoy his time there even more by spending it being active outdoors with his peers. One weekend in August, he signed up for a daylong sports camp that provided tennis instruction in the morning and golf in the afternoon. He returned home at the end of the day utterly smitten with golf.

We were so thrilled by Matt's enthusiasm that we enrolled in a family golf clinic so the three of us could learn and play together. We were all beginners, out there to have fun and enjoy the beauty of the Blue Ridge Mountains. We passed many a delightful afternoon playing nine holes. With a tee time late in the day and no one behind us on the course, we could take our time, observing the privilege of unlimited mulligans (do-overs) and stopping to harvest lost golf balls in the woods. Advancing the little white ball down the fairway to the little white cup was always secondary to having a good time.

Until I switched to a consulting firm where golf was not a hobby but a responsibility. One of the benefits—nay, expectations—of being a partner in this firm was that I would play golf with my colleagues and clients. In fact, I would be expected to woo prospective clients on the golf course. To do that, I was expected to be a moderately good golfer, not an embarrassment to my firm and myself.

Gone were the leisurely afternoons on my beloved Blue Ridge golf course. Now my games with family became practice for the performance my partners expected me to deliver. While swearing was not the norm for me, now when I missed the first two shots off the tee, I swore. Now when I hit a shot into a sand trap, I threw my club down the fairway while swearing. When this happened, I'd explain to my companions that my father had been in the merchant marines. They'd say, "Did he swear a lot?" "No," I'd reply, "evidently it skipped a generation."

Because children don't do what we say but rather do what they see *us* do, it's unsurprising that, in short order, my eleven-year-old was also throwing his clubs and swearing like a sailor. That's when I finally got a grip. Matt and I agreed that when either of us behaved badly on the course, we had to take a time-out together in the golf cart until both of us had returned to civility. As a result, Matt and I went through a period where we spent more time in the golf cart than on the course. This may have been just as well, because we were living proof that anger is not necessarily a performance enhancer.

One day, weary of swearing, throwing clubs, and spending

time in the cart, the two of us sat there, arms crossed, scowling. After a few minutes of reflection, I said, "Babe, this has got to stop. Neither of us is having any fun anymore. I think I've figured out my problem. I'm imagining the potentially angry, ridiculing voices of my partners in my head, and I can't relax and have fun when I've put them in there to beat me up. What's going on in your head?" He looked at me with all the disgust of a kid who believes his parent has gone 'round the bend and said, "I have no idea. I don't even know your new partners!"

Here is the essence of what I have learned from nearly sixty years on this earth. The nugget, the kernel, the gem. The only hope for finding peace in this life—not just comfort but deep abiding peace—is to be insatiably, fearlessly curious about myself.

Not just the attractive ways I show up—my kindness, compassion, wisdom, generosity, and humor. It is important for me to acknowledge those things, but it is not enough. I need to be endlessly inquisitive about *all* of it, especially the unattractive habits—my insensitivity, impatience, obsession, bitterness, anger, anxiety, and despair. I have grown the most and found deep abiding peace only by embracing the ugly parts as well: appalling thoughts, speech, and behavior. It all matters and must be considered in the mix—the good, the bad, the pretty, and the ugly. All of it acknowledged with courage, compassion, and love. This concoction of disparate and dissonant motivations and behaviors is what it means to be human.

We are all capable of the full range of human motivations and behaviors; none of us is exempt. Refusing to see any part of it, lulling myself into oblivion by clinging to an incomplete, distorted Polly Perfect self-image always leads to my undoing. The greater and deeper the denial, the longer and harder the fall because that which is denied will wreak havoc. Maybe not today or tomorrow. But the longer I look without seeing and hear without listening, the more I stand to lose.

The great irony is that I'm the only person fooled when I deny the full truth of how I show up. I broadcast it through what I say and when I am silent. Through the actions I take and the times I fail to act. Through what I cherish and what I reject. Through what I long for and what I fear. I am the only one kept in the dark by living a life of denial about myself.

One of the greatest gifts I can give anyone is having the honesty and courage to see and share myself fully so that we both might benefit from our shared insight, compassion, and good humor—failures, resilience, victories. We are here to help each other grow by sharing without reservation the only thing we have to give—our authentic selves.

The only person controlling your life is *you*! Choose your energy and change your life. If you want to keep making yourself miserable and continue contaminating the energy of every situation you encounter, stop reading this book and keep doing what you're doing. But if you have had enough, if you are ready to stop the insanity, keep reading. You are going to love what happens when you learn to embrace the next aspect of love: compassion.

Compassion
I acknowledge and value my feelings.

Compassion is not sympathy. Sympathy is laced with judging because it involves *feeling sorry for someone*. However well intentioned, sympathy is a form of judging based in determining that whatever is happening to you or someone else shouldn't be happening. Yet some of the greatest growth opportunities in life come through very painful experiences.

Compassion is *feeling with someone*. Being a loving, respectful, fully present, nondirective, nonjudging companion who holds a sacred space in which the pained one can be present and completely authentic. True compassion is a rare experience. So often, sharing our pain with another person results in them trying to

- get us to deny it (*it's not real*);
- convince us to ignore it (*it's not that bad*);
- focus our attention on something else (*it's not worth it*); or
- fix it for us (*it's so bad, it needs to stop right now, and you're so inept, I'll have to do it for you*).

Compassion, on the other hand, is grounded in believing with every fiber of your being that we are each doing the best we can in every moment with the love and light we are able to access at that time, given the blocks resulting from whatever fears we still choose to carry.

If any of you are still harboring the illusion that those of us in the "helping professions" are able to help others because we are totally self-actualized; always have it all together; never get confused, sad, angry, frustrated, needy, or pushy; and never sink into bottomless despair, then you need to reread the previous sections.

Those of us in the helping professions are able to help others precisely *because* we have grappled with similar challenges in our own lives. We are able to help because we have

- been overwhelmed by the associated pain (rage, frustration, confusion, doubt, anxiety, depression, etc.);
- not prevailed immediately (flopped around in the mire of despair more than a few times for more than a few minutes); and
- had amazing grace dawn yet again.

I have come to understand that, in many cases, when I think I'm demonstrating *empathy* for someone, it's really *sympathy*. When I demonstrate empathy, I feel sorry *with* the other person. My ability to put myself in that person's place is directly proportional to my ability to feel and identify the full range of my own emotions. With *sympathy*, because I'm not aware of having ever felt anything like what that person is feeling, the most I can do is feel sorry *for* her. Sorry she had to go through whatever trial was currently beating her face-first into the dirt. Sometimes in the throes of *sympathy*, when I was feeling a bit too smug about my own more highly evolved consciousness (come on, you've all been *there*), I would say to myself (or heaven help me, say aloud), "Gee, it's a shame Susie doesn't know all that I know. Then she wouldn't still be grieving her husband's death or abandonment by her seventeen-year life partner or the potential loss of her home or the death of her beloved animal companion or the promotion she didn't get at work or whatever. If Susie was as wise as I am, it wouldn't have hit her so hard to begin with, she'd certainly be over it by now, and she would be returned to the perpetually happy fold of the incredibly enlightened."

There's a reason Pema Chödrön warns against "spiritual

arrogance"—becoming too comfortable with how well we are doing on the path to enlightenment. The point of enlightenment is not to become superior and feel no pain. It is to open your heart wider to your own pain and, through that experience, to the pain of others. It's to help you develop deeper love and true empathy for yourself and everyone else. It's so you can finally connect to all of humankind on the most profound level by understanding we are one.

Many of us in the helping professions are referred to as wounded healers because what we have chosen to do with our healed wounds is dedicate our lives to helping others heal and grow. The most inspiring healers and teachers, certainly the ones nearest and dearest to me, are comfortable being candid concerning their particular wounds (abandonment, burnout, addiction, depression, and more). By sharing openly their struggles, defeats, and victories, wounded healers help others open to the possibility that if one of us can prevail, maybe all of us can. In the movie *Leap of Faith*, Liam Neeson (the local sheriff) is exposing Steve Martin (traveling revivalist extraordinaire) as a fraud, based on evidence of Martin's criminal record from a young age. Neeson thinks this *disqualifies* Martin to lead others to a better life. Martin replies that, au contraire, herein lies his chief qualification. Who are you going to trust to lead you out of the mess you've made of your life? The upright guy who has always walked the straight and narrow or the man who found redemption after wallowing in the muck and mire?

The one thing we can be certain of—in addition to death and taxes—is that, no matter what, we are all human. Whenever we start to forget that, start to get just the least bit clueless or cocky, the Universe has a not-so-funny way of reminding us—through yet another spectacular crash and burn—that we still have much left to learn about compassion.

Our reactions to our own pain are no exception. Here the full range of our most uncompassionate responses gets regular exercise. While it can be difficult to just *be* with another who is in pain, learning to do so is key to healthy processing of the many forms of grieving we encounter in life. The ability to hold sacred space is as vital to unconditional *self*-love as it is to loving another.

While understanding these concepts intellectually is a necessary starting point, it's not sufficient to deliver substantial, sustainable results. For these lessons to have a lasting impact, they must go from something you think sounds logical and interesting to something you live at all times as your own personal truth. If you stop with respect and curiosity, you will miss the full potential impact of unconditional love. Without compassion, love *cannot* be fully expressed. Fear will retain a foothold. Curiosity without compassion can quickly shift to judging that leads directly back to fear-based disrespect. Whether that judging takes the form of sympathy or trying to fix it, judging will pull you out of unconditional love and plant you firmly back in the land of fear.

Noticing and embracing all of our emotions is essential to finding flow and making it a way of life. It is nearly impossible to know how to nurture ourselves optimally if we are not willing to go inside, root around a bit, and discover what makes us tick.

I know that when you are going through something painful you might feel you can't bear the added anguish that might result from additional data. The opposite is actually the case; the fear festers and grows in the dark, taking over our lives precisely because we refuse to look at it closely. When we expose it to light and air by examining it with love, respect, curiosity, compassion, and gratitude rather than judging, the fear immediately begins to lose some of its power.

Emotions are important messengers. They help us notice the implications of what is happening and gain the maximum benefit from everything we experience. They are powerful indicators of where fear may still have a stronghold and be blocking our growth. They point the way to where we might go exploring for untapped veins of developmental gold.

Knowing how to recognize, process, express, and release emotions is essential to our well-being. When we don't do so, the resulting buildup of fear-based emotional toxins can be energetically lethal. Our systems bog down from the poison, and we become stuck in an endless loop of replaying past pain, injuring and crippling ourselves even more.

When I first began coaching, I was surprised by the number of clients, men and women alike, who were ashamed of crying, even in the presence of a licensed professional coach. Some cited a special appreciation for the norm of coaching by phone because they believed I wouldn't know when they were crying. (Though it is unlikely that an experienced, intuitive life coach won't know that you are crying, even if you do so silently.) Tears are a common human response to strong emotion, especially fear and its cousins. For many, the only way to avoid crying is to avoid feeling.

Why is shedding tears so important and beneficial? There is a great parallel in the example of therapeutic massage. Every massage therapist I've ever worked with encouraged me to drink lots of water for the twenty-four to forty-eight hours after a massage. Deep tissue work releases copious toxins into your system. For the net result of the massage to be beneficial, it is necessary to flush those toxins from your system as quickly and completely as possible. When you don't do so, your body may become overwhelmed, resulting in illness. Water is an essential element in ensuring that the massage is therapeutic and not detrimental. Water fosters flow.

Think of crying as the emotional equivalent of water after a massage. When you've done deep emotional work on your own or with a guide, stored emotional toxins are released into your system. Tears are one of the common ways to release those toxins and gain the full benefit of the emotional work. Some clients who are carrying a lifetime of unacknowledged, unfelt stored emotions say they are afraid that if they start crying now, they will never stop. While I empathize with that concern, I am happy to report it doesn't tend to happen. Even a little bit of crying can do a world of good. The stored-up tears do stop, and then, by remaining aware and fully embracing all of your feelings all of the time, you'll find a little bit of crying goes a long way. Just respecting your feelings enough to notice them and demonstrate compassion rather than continuing to tell yourself to suck it up and stop being a wimp will result in far greater emotional equilibrium and resilience in the face of life's ups and downs.

When tears arise, it's an indicator that we are in the presence of a big insight that bears deeper exploration once the strong emotions have been respected and cleared. Other times, there is nothing of note, just a need for a little release of pent-up stress. How do you know which you are dealing with?

Once the tears have passed, breathe, close your eyes, and

recenter yourself. Once centered, ask yourself if something bears deeper examination. Notice subtle responses throughout the major energy systems in your body, especially any tightening in your head, neck, chest, solar plexus, or stomach. Such responses may mean there is more to be worked through. An overall feeling of well-being usually means there is nothing to look at, or nothing to look at right now. In all cases, just trust your intuition. This powerful technique may also be applied to decision making. While it may feel too subtle to notice at first, with practice you will become quite adept at reading your energy.

To help anchor this learning about compassion in reality, I will share an example of how this shows up in my relationship with myself. My illustration is not a recipe for the only method that works; it is an example of what often works for me, a way for you to get started and, with some curiosity and experimentation, figure out what works best for you.

My name, Deborah, means "the bee" in Hebrew, as in "busy as a bee" (how unsurprising). My muse and inner child is named Bee. How do I know that's her name? She told me. You will learn more about that process and the role of the muse on your personal board of directors in chapter 6. My pet name for Bee is Little Bee or Bumble Bee.

As with any healthy, meaningful relationship, I check in with her regularly. I don't just wait until I sense something is amiss. When I do notice discomfort arising, which often shows up as a tightening in my chest or heart chakra, I stop what I'm doing, place my hand over my heart, breathe deeply, and lovingly say, "What is it, Little Bee? I'm right here. You're not alone."

If circumstances permit, I find this dialogue is most effective conducted out loud. My guess is that engaging speech and hearing along with touch and thinking helps amplify the experience so I can access what's happening more deeply and process it more effectively and fully. Honestly, it doesn't really matter to me *why* it works, just *that* it works. I am an intuitive life coach; while I respect reason, I never trust it over intuition. Why would I use a lower level of knowledge to override a much higher form of wisdom?

Back to Little Bee. "I know you're in pain. Tell me what it's about." I stop and listen. Trusting my intuition again, whatever comes up, that's where I go in. As my inner creative wild child and muse, she usually starts with the idea that I'm working her too hard and she's not had any fun in a while. She abhors drudgery and forced labor. Many times, I'll pat my shoulder gently as I would a beloved child and say, "I know, Little One. You've been working long hours. Your creativity has been such a big help. Thanks to your contribution, the writing is going to be so much more enjoyable and effective in helping as many people as possible find hope and learn to love themselves. I couldn't do it without you. I also understand that you cannot give anything of lasting value from an empty well. You really need to take a break and refresh yourself. To rest and restock your creative juices with some fun activities so you'll be able to continue to contribute. Tell me what you'd like to do, and we'll make a specific plan for how and when we're going to do it."

At this point, I won't take you through all the ins and outs of how this dialogue might go. Sometimes there's a lengthy and entertaining negotiation. Sometimes all Bee needs is for me to take a five-minute break and visit the loo. A glass of water or mug of tea. A little snack if it's been a while since I ate. Turning on the electric fireplace and adding a sweater because the room had gotten cold two hours ago but my guardian Ella (also explained in chapter 6) was so heads down in the writing that she never noticed. Or Ella had noticed but didn't want me to stop to address my physical discomfort because she worried that if I stopped, the flow of words wouldn't return, an example of fear-based scarcity mentality at work.

The process of connecting with Bee's (which is to say that aspect of my own) thoughts and feelings is to stop, focus my attention, set my intention, go in, ask respectfully, listen deeply, explore, demonstrate compassion, and figure out what to do. Funny thing is, usually all she needs is something small, not a Mercedes or a yacht. A trip to the bathroom, a glass of water, a piece of cheese, a cat to pet, a peek out the window to appreciate the Rocky Mountains, or a walk around her yard to breathe fresh air and feel the sun on her face for a few minutes.

Then Bee will go back to work with me happily, knowing she is free, she matters, and she is powerful. A forced march is never the answer to a quality outcome. Force results in mental exhaustion, emotional deterioration, and output that's less than optimal. Giving myself regular breaks fosters a sense of flow and produces spectacular results. I *can* trust myself to complete the work when the time is right.

Occasionally, when I talk with Little Bee, tears erupt, and I find a surprisingly deep pain. Something that I ignored for far too long until it inflicted real damage. Then I know it is time to stop, put everything else on hold, and give it my full attention. There is always time for the things that matter. Our only responsibility in each moment is to discern what matters most right now, to focus, and to follow through. My thoughts and feelings always matter, especially if I know they are causing me pain.

We began this chapter focused on unconditional love, with respect, curiosity, and compassion as important aspects for defining what that sort of love looks like. In the last section of this chapter, we will explore gratitude, the final aspect of love and the key to fostering flow.

Gratitude

I appreciate my life; everything is an opportunity.

I first became acquainted with the idea of a gratitude practice in 1995 through Sarah Ban Breathnach's book *Simple Abundance*. The book's core concept was to begin and end each day by naming at least five things for which I was grateful. Some days the list overflowed with twenty-five or more items, evidence of my consciousness of the generosity of the Universe. Other days, when I perceived things as going poorly, I struggled to identify even five things for which I was thankful.

I followed the gratitude practice off and on through the years but abandoned it entirely at the very time when I could have most benefited from it. When I got insanely, stressfully busy in the final years of my consulting career, I left the gratitude practice by the side of the road, having erroneously concluded that I was too busy to be intentionally grateful.

Fast forward to 2010, when I had retired, lost eighty pounds, escaped depression, and began pursuing my calling as a life coach and Reiki master, teaching others about the transformative power of falling in love with themselves. Though love, respect, curiosity, and compassion were serving me well in manifesting unconditional self-love, sometimes when my life became especially complex, the judging voice could still take over with its fear-based messages of doom and gloom.

One day, during written meditation, I remembered the power of my former gratitude practice and wondered if it might be the missing link. As I went beyond just a morning and evening event to making it a way of life I call *radical gratitude*, here is what I discovered.

Love and gratitude serve as the bookends of constructive core energy. Between them, they encompass and support all the other aspects of love: respect, curiosity, and compassion. Love initiates the flow of core energy; gratitude expands it. Love is the originator. Gratitude is the catalyst. Through the eyes of gratitude, we see that *everything is an opportunity,* a grace-filled gift of Universal love characterized by loving-kindness, elegant beauty, copious generosity, and infinite mercy.

Radical gratitude fosters a life of generous, effortless, gracious flow filled with faith, hope, prosperity, peace, and joy.

- **Faith:** I am confident that love is the greatest power in the Universe.
- **Hope:** Universal love is always unfolding the highest good for all, in all, through all.
- **Prosperity:** My Universal Source is excellent, limitless, and reliable.
- **Peace:** I relax into all that was, is, and will be.
- **Joy:** Whatever my circumstances, I know *who* I am and *Whose* I am: a unique cocreative expression of the Divine.

What might radical gratitude look like in real life? Let's start with the example of cleaning the litter boxes for my three beloved cats, SiddhaLee, Mortimer, and Maisy Jane. My feline family members are far from aloof. They are my constant companions, comforters, playmates, greatest teachers, and—no kidding—coaching assistants. If you are interested in hearing more about their role in holding client-specific sacred space during coaching, visit my VoiceAmerica host page at tiny.cc/djwradio and listen to the recording of the

January 6, 2013 episode of my weekly radio show, starting at the thirty-one-minute mark.

As anyone who has ever been owned by a cat can tell you, cats require litter boxes. To function effectively, there needs to be at least one more litter box than the number of cats, and those boxes need to be kept clean. With experimentation, I discovered that, ever the overachievers, my *three* cats require *six* boxes that need to be scooped free of any refuse morning and night. Those six boxes also need to be emptied completely of all litter, washed out, and replaced with fresh litter once a month.

As the number of litter boxes escalated, at first I was resentful. Why couldn't they stop being so territorial and use fewer boxes? I perceived the money and time I was investing as excessive and burdensome. Until, a year after he came to live with me, my Mortimer became ill and nearly died. When we pulled him back from the brink of death and he began to grow stronger, it finally hit me: cleaning litter boxes is an act of love. It is a privilege and honor to be able to return a fraction of the love and companionship he and his mates shower on me daily, by handling this hygiene task for them. A funny thing happened; when I chose to shift my energy from resentment to gratitude, litter patrol was no longer a burden. Now I sing and chatter happily to the cats while I move from room to room, ever their faithful, itinerant scooper.

Let's extend the example to more mundane fare. When I was a young child, I never even dreamed of a miraculous machine that would wash and dry the dishes for me so that all I had to do was put them away. Then we got our first dishwasher. Things were great for the first few months, but then I began taking my new blessing for granted, and before you know it, my brother and I were fighting over who was putting away more dishes and what could be done about it. Not an example of gratitude. Even as an adult, I still found I had days when I grumbled about how much I had to do and how long it took to empty the dishwasher. Now, when I apply the gratitude principle, putting the dishes away is easy, fast, and fun. How cool to have a machine that washes and dries them for me.

This week, I started the dishwasher just before settling down at my kitchen table for my morning meditation. A few minutes later, I realized how comforted I was by the gentle thrumming and splashing sounds of the elixir of life, water, cleansing my life of residue, reminding me that each day, each moment, offers the opportunity for a fresh start. Who knew a dishwasher could be the source of meditative insight? When we choose to look at everything through the lens of gratitude, our perspective is always rose-colored by appreciation.

Speaking of gratitude for technology, how cool is it that I have a computer, printer, and wireless network right in my own home? How could I have ever complained when the printer ran out of ink in the middle of a big job and I *had to* replace the cartridges? Or my cellphone signal didn't work so well in the Ozarks? I remember the days when there were no color TVs, personal computers, printers, or cell phones. Now, when any of my technology hits a bump in the road, I repeat an affirmation I learned from Louise L. Hay many years ago, one that still strikes me as funny and so has the added benefit of making me laugh aloud: "Cars and refrigerators do not break down when we are in a good place." So when things *do* break down, and I catch myself grumbling, I set my intention to align myself with a better place (gratitude) so I'll quit wasting my energy in whining and do something constructive (like replacing the empty ink cartridge).

The day after writing this section on gratitude, the Universe sent me a technology "refresher" lesson in the form of twenty-four hours in which it appeared my most recent two years of Quicken financial data had become corrupted beyond repair. I repeatedly practiced deep breathing and clearing myself of all fear throughout the process. This allowed me to access my deepest wisdom and discover the key to resolving the seeming "problem" when even Quicken advanced tech support had given up. Ta-da! It would appear I've learned the technology lesson now. Enough with the pop quizzes already!

So many things to be grateful for: clean water; hot showers; healthcare; education; heat in the winter and air conditioning in the summer; healthy food; smiles, hugs, and kisses; and physical, mental, emotional, and spiritual abilities.

When I stay centered in gratitude for all of life's simple blessings, I find it easier to stay anchored there in the more painful times. The friend who dumps me. The spouse who becomes ill. The hurricane that devastates the beloved South Jersey Shore of my childhood. The movie theater mass shooting in my hometown of Aurora, Colorado. Being present in New York City on September 11, 2001, where I spent the night accounting for my missing consulting colleagues. When viewed through the lens of gratitude, even those painful experiences are opportunities for deeper insight, greater compassion, dramatic personal growth, and increased appreciation for the gift of life. In the words of the great sage Kahlil Gibran, "Wake at dawn with a winged heart and give thanks for another day of loving."

The Principle of Circulation

As I wrap up this initial discussion of gratitude, I want to explore an essential aspect of *genuine* gratitude that *truly* fosters flow: the principle of circulation. While many people are extremely comfortable with *giving to others*, far fewer are equally comfortable with *receiving from others*. Raised with "It is better to give than receive" and "God loveth a cheerful giver," many have mistakenly concluded that life is all about giving. But giving without a similar commitment to receiving *blocks* rather than fosters flow.

Flow requires free circulation, both inflow and outflow, with neither condition being desired, admired, or sought after more than the other. Giving with abandon accompanied by resistance to receiving is *not* what love looks like and it won't encourage flow. Such duality indicates that fear has crept in and tainted what could, if fueled differently, be an act of love. The roots of this sort of circulation imbalance are planted firmly in misunderstanding the nature of power and assuming power is the same thing as force.

The misperception is based in the belief that giving will put me in the "up" position, leaving me superior and powerful. Once I succeed in giving to you, I can expect you to return the favor on demand in the future in whatever form I desire consistent with my unilateral terms and conditions.

With this definition of giving in place, it follows that I might perceive *receiving* would put me in the "down" position, leaving me inferior and powerless. Once I succumb to receiving from you, I will be obligated and vulnerable to acting for your benefit in the future—on demand and against my will—in ways that may conflict with my personal values and abilities.

The simple recalibration to these misperceptions is to realize *that* sort of exchange is not what love looks like. Rereading the previous sections on love's essential attributes of respect, curiosity, and compassion will increase your clarity in that regard. As the giver, when you choose love as your core fuel, whatever the expectations of the receiver, you *never* give from a desire to control or manipulate others. And as the receiver, when you choose love as your core fuel, whatever the expectations of the giver, you are never obligated to respond from fear. Only you decide what is right for your life. What you give and receive, when, why, how, and how much are always yours to choose. In each moment, you have the opportunity to choose love over fear and behave in alignment with your choice.

Here's an additional insight to help you move more comfortably into balance, harmony, and understanding concerning the roles of giving and receiving in fostering flow. The practice of "over-giving" is just another variation on the arrogance-based disrespectful interference we explored in the section on respect. When we over-give, we rob the recipient of the opportunity to develop the healthy independence essential to personal growth and freedom. How do you know when this is the case? As always, look underneath your potential actions and be unflinchingly honest with yourself about whether your core fuel is love or fear. Once you recognize your fuel, you have the opportunity to respect yourself and the other by making a conscious constructive choice.

People sometimes respond to this perspective on giving and receiving by saying, "But Deborah, it just feels so good to give!" Yes, it does feel good. And when you refuse to *receive* with gratitude and grace, you rob another of experiencing that joy of giving. Much as you may not like to admit it, such behavior demonstrates greediness: hoarding all of that good feeling for yourself. When you give but don't embrace receiving, you imprison yourself with fear and your gifts become tainted.

Remember to consider the big picture when assessing how well circulation is working in your life. Don't expect direct reciprocity in relation to what you give. Adopt a "pay it forward" mindset and the God's-eye view, knowing that the circulation you set in motion when you give to a friend or stranger, may return to you in ways you never dreamed of through people you don't even know. When you celebrate giving *and* receiving with a sense of joy and freedom, you exhibit genuine gratitude and foster for yourself and others lives of generous, effortless, gracious flow filled with faith, hope, prosperity, peace, and joy.

Core Energy Scan

Now that you have greater understanding of the roles of love, respect, curiosity, compassion, and gratitude in fostering constructive core energy and manifesting a life of flow, you are better equipped to notice when any one of the big five would benefit from recalibration and what form that might take.

Core Energy Scan

I approach life with love, respect, curiosity, and compassion, revealing and advancing the highest good.
My gratitude for Universal abundance anchors each moment
in generous, effortless, gracious flow filled with faith, hope, prosperity, peace, and joy.

	FEAR	Indicators of Insufficiency		LOVE	Baby Steps to Strengthen My Reality
CONTEMPT	Discord Irritation Conflict Separation Destruction Abandonment		RESPECT	Harmony Patience Peace Oneness Construction Loyalty	
JUDGING	Anger Obstruction Worry Despair Constriction Doubt		CURIOSITY	Serenity Flow Faith Hope Expansion Trust	
SHAME	Abuse Cruelty Neglect Disapproval Rejection Blame		COMPASSION	Nurturing Kindness Consideration Encouragement Acceptance Forgiveness	
LACK	Exhaustion Depletion Poverty Stinginess Scarcity Misery		GRATITUDE	Invigoration Renewal Prosperity Generosity Abundance Joy	

© DJW Life Coach LLC 2012

Figure 5: Core Energy Scan

Figure 5 provides a simple form to guide this process. The scan consists of a five-step process, with each step grounded in caring enough about yourself to do the following:

- Pay attention so that you notice quickly whenever fear creeps into your energetic mix.
- Invest your energy in assessing the root cause of the fear.
- Determine what baby steps will strengthen the presence of love in your reality.
- Hold yourself accountable for following through on your commitment to take action.
- Assess your results and continuously refine and expand your action plan to maximize the presence of love and minimize the presence of fear in the core energy with which you fuel your life.

You are worth the effort. With practice, you will turn unconditional self-love into a healthy new habit that will become a way of life. When love takes over your core energy, you will begin building the less stressful, more fulfilling life you dream of.

Energy Leadership Index Assessment

I am often asked why I have chosen to make completing iPEC's Energy Leadership Index (ELI) assessment integral to my life coaching approach. The answer is simple: embracing the principles and insights of this tool delivers life-transforming results.

Energy Leadership refers to a unique process of leading your energy so it works for you rather than against you. By applying the principles of Energy Leadership, you can increase your ability to shift your own energy and the energy of those around you. When you do that, you will help inspire and motivate yourself and others, feel a greater sense of purpose, and get more done with much less effort and stress.

The ELI is a life attitude assessment based on an energy/action model. It reveals how the thoughts, emotions, and behaviors you choose are affecting the energy you live with in every moment, which in turn affects the results you get. It measures your level of energy based on your attitude—your perception of and perspective on your world. Because attitude is subjective, it is also malleable.

As a certified professional coach and ELI master practitioner, I help you apply the principles of Energy Leadership and your ELI results to alter your attitude, change your perspective, shift your consciousness, increase your energy, and enhance your leadership effectiveness, personally and professionally.

We've laid a firm foundation for a life of flow with core energy fueled by love, respect, curiosity, compassion, and gratitude. Next, through sensory balance, we will build the day-to-day infrastructure to keep your life of flow securely grounded.

For more insights into the role of core energy, read *Energy Leadership* by Bruce D. Schneider.

Chapter 5:
Creating Balance—
Feeding Your Nine Senses

Like the framing in a home, our outer and inner senses build on our energetic foundation to provide the day-to-day infrastructure for a life of flow securely grounded in constructive core energy. Sensory balance involves feeding all of our senses in healthy, balanced ways so that no one sense takes over trying to fill voids it can never hope to fill. This begins with mindfully feeding our five outer senses, through which we celebrate our world, and it extends to intentionally feeding our four inner senses of creativity, vitality, spirituality, and belonging, through which we imbue our experience with meaning.

Outer Senses—I
Celebrate My World

Though the nine senses overlap and interact freely to enrich our experience, for simplicity we'll explore them one at a time, beginning with the outer senses. What role might balanced feeding of your outer senses play in finding flow and the Journey to Wholeness?

Using the terms of the Discovery Framework, the outer senses are like the roof and outer walls of our energetic home (figure 6). They are an invaluable interface for interaction with the external world. Built on the firm foundation of constructive core energy, when functioning optimally, they are able to transmit and incorporate what will serve the highest good while filtering out what is not beneficial.

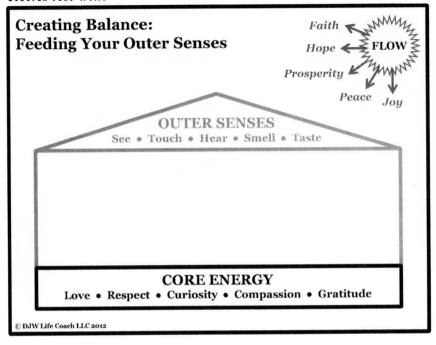

Figure 6: Outer Senses

See

A vast cornucopia of sights—color, pattern, movement, people, places, objects—expands my possibilities.

Feeding your sense of sight starts by surrounding yourself with colors, patterns, and objects that please your eye. Do you prefer variety or consistency? As an artist, I love every color in every shade imaginable. I use all of them in my art and my environments, but my favorite colors are purple, orange, and green. It's uncanny how often they end up in my art, in my living space, and on my body without any conscious intention. In fact, even when I try to exclude them in a design, they sneak in no matter what.

Why? When I did some research, I learned that different colors vibrate at different frequencies and resonate to different themes and moods. If you are intrigued by the connections between color, energy, and mood, you will find copious opinions on the Internet and at the library. Figure 7 shows my quick version of how colors align with the chakras, or energetic substations of the body.

CHAKRA SUMMARY

Chakra	Focus	Colors
7 Crown	Oneness, Spirituality, Divine Wisdom	Purple, White
6 Third Eye	Reason, Intuition, Discernment	Dark Blue
5 Throat	Choices, Self-Expression	Bright Blue, Light Blue
4 Heart	Love, Compassion, Self-Acceptance, Saying Yes	Green
3 Solar Plexus	Courage, Self-Esteem, Vitality, Saying No	Yellow
2 Sacral	Joy, Play, Relationships, Creativity, Flexibility	Orange
1 Root	Stability, Belonging, Self-Preservation	Black, Brown, Red, Pink

© DJW Life Coach LLC 2012

Figure 7: Chakra Summary

Purple, orange, and green represent spirituality, creativity, and love, respectively. In combination, they feed my soul. Pale tints in spring, bright hues in summer, dusty tones in fall, and darker shades in winter, they are always present. They comfort and delight me, providing a feeling of consistency and wholeness. What we love about the colors is not the colors themselves. It's how we feel when we see them. That is true of all the senses. We don't enjoy the *stimuli*; we enjoy how we *feel* in their presence.

Color affinities can be both indicators and influencers of our moods and intentions. As with most things, I begin by following my intuition and then, if my energy is flat or cloudy, I'll apply reason and intention. Let's use my eyeglasses as an example. I have five pair in five different colors. (Two are variations on purple. How unsurprising.) My glasses are often the first "clothing" choice of the day. Sometimes I just reach for a color instinctively and find that my clothing colors align. When I translate my intuitive color choice to the frequencies of the chakras, it's uncanny how often what I choose fits perfectly with where I need rebalancing or a boost. For example, I instinctively pick my bright blue eyeglasses on a day when I have a lot of writing or public speaking on my agenda. In chakra terms, bright blue resonates to self-expression energy.

Other times, when no strong color is drawing me, I'll reason out which colors I should include based on where my energy needs realigning or fortifying. Although the process may sound complicated, it actually takes only a few moments.

Changes in color affinities sometimes signal major events and shifts in direction. For example, as I completed my two iPEC coaching certifications, I was less consistently drawn to purple, orange, and green and often attracted to turquoise (self-expression), yellow (self-esteem), and bright pink (identity). I didn't resist, just relaxed into this new color phase of my life and enjoyed the broader range of experience.

Clothing is your portable environment. While I may be especially attuned to it as a fashion artist, it affects all of us. Clothing is the house we wear on our bodies and carry around all day. Try beginning each day by consciously selecting clothing that supports you in expressing how you want to show up that day.

An individual item may nurture multiple senses. While I've started by exploring a single outer sense, you can quickly see how interrelated they are. For example, clothing nurtures our senses of sight and touch.

Let's expand our perspective beyond feeding ourselves with colors to include feeding ourselves with images and symbols. As you know by now, I love cats and live with three—SiddhaLee, Mortimer, and Maisy Jane. To be more accurate, they let me live in *their* house, sleep in *their* king-size bed, eat in *their* kitchen, and work in *their* office. We're crazy about each other. I love the way it feels to be with cats. I foster that feeling by maximizing the opportunities to experience it. I season my environment liberally with images of cats—pictures, quilts, jewelry, and more.

I also love the symbolism of butterflies—patience and hope for the fertile possibilities of life transformation during incubation in a dark void. Their images are sprinkled liberally throughout my life, including serving as my primary life coaching logo. I love dragonflies—symbols of living in the moment, abandoning self-limiting beliefs, seeing the vast potential of the Universe, and the power and poise that come with the mental and emotional maturity of seeing the deeper meaning to life. I adore books too—the power of human thought shared. I love seeing them in my space, reminding me that even when I sit alone writing, I am not alone. I am surrounded by every person who has ever had an idea or experience and felt compelled to share it with someone else for the benefit of reader and author.

In the world of entertainment, pay attention to what you read and watch; the themes and messages affect your energy. Are you feeding yourself a visual diet of optimism and unlimited possibilities (love) or pessimism and scarcity (fear)? I have become very selective about books, movies, and television shows. My test for choosing what I consume is, "Will watching or reading this expand and strengthen my ability to fulfill my purpose or limit and weaken it?"

Don't get hung up on my colors and choice of symbols; the point is to figure out the colors and images to which you resonate. While there are many books on standard energetic reactions to colors (blue is soothing, yellow is cheerful, red is energizing or irritating, black is depressing or stabilizing, etc.), we are not interested in *standard* reactions. What matters here is your *personal* reaction. Experiment and determine what unique mix is most beneficial in helping you live in flow.

Provide a pleasing visual meal in each room. Pay attention to portion control, avoiding the visual version of gluttony by overwhelming your senses with too much stimulation and thereby numbing them. Go for healthy, digestible meals that leave you hungry an hour later for more visual stimulation outside your home and work location. Include regular outings to places that augment your visual diet with special treats: botanical gardens, galleries, the mountains, book stores, pet shops, the ocean, museums, fabric shops, art supply stores—whatever delights *you*. I have a client who feeds her sense of sight by selecting fresh produce based on including as many colors as possible, which also happens to be very good for you nutritionally. On other grocery shopping escapades, she focuses on what smells good together, demonstrating once again the opportunity to have a single item nurture more than one sense at a time.

I've explored the sense of sight in some detail to give you a feel for what's involved. I will provide briefer descriptions for each of the remaining outer senses and leave it to you to fill in your personal details.

Touch

A broad range of tactile stimuli—hot, cold, soft, hard, wet, dry, smooth, rough, fuzzy, furry, fluffy—intensifies my experiences.

Let's begin with temperature. Do you prefer feeling warm or cool, or does it vary? While there are many upsides physically, mentally, emotionally, and spiritually to losing eighty pounds, there is one downside: I often feel cold, and I don't like it. I want to feel warm and dry all year round. Over time, I realized feeling cold didn't just have a negative physical effect on me. That chill extended to my mental, emotional, and spiritual state. For me, feeling cold resonates with deprivation, which vibrates with fear. So I live in a state of constant mindfulness concerning temperature. I always have with me many options for layering my clothing based on the environmental variations I may encounter during my day. While my delightful home state of Colorado boasts more than three hundred sunny days a year, it can experience wild temperature swings throughout any given day at any time of year.

I also invested in little electric fireplaces in the main rooms of my home. They are an inexpensive, attractive, and highly functional method of easily adjusting the temperature to nurture my body, mind, heart, and soul.

It took me a while to figure out where the potential thermostatic issues might occur and what to do about them. For example, in restaurants in the summer, I have learned to order iced tea with no ice (which is to say warm or room temperature tea). In the winter, no matter where I am, I always have a hot cup of something at hand.

You may be one of those people who are always too warm, so you will be identifying ways to lower the temperature of your environment. Or your preferences may vary from warm to cool based on your season, activity, or mood. My husband likes to be warm in the winter and cool in the summer, but he *always* drinks his beverages nearly frozen. The point is to be curious about what feels good to you, respectful enough to notice how you're feeling, compassionate enough to do something about it, and grateful for the opportunity to fine-tune your environment.

The same applies when it comes to the texture of your world. Clothing, furniture, bedding, flooring—each of these bring opportunities to explore what feels good to you and, to the best of your abilities, align your world with what you find optimal.

There are many more opportunities to nurture yourself by feeding your sense of touch: therapeutic massage, a hug, a hot shower, caressing the soft coat of your animal companion, a warm whirlpool bath, and rich body lotions to name just a few. If the lotions are scented, they offer the bonus of also feeding your sense of smell. Two of the most meaningful ways I demonstrate the depth of my love for myself take a total of ninety seconds a day. In the morning, after my shower, before drying off, I apply baby oil to my still wet body. It's a quick, inexpensive, and incredibly effective method of sealing moisture into my skin. And morning and night, no matter how busy or tired I am, I always massage rich beautifully scented body cream into my feet before putting on my socks. These acts are my way of appreciating and pampering myself. My feet do so much to support and transport me; it seems a small repayment of the debt I owe them. This ritual doesn't just nourish my skin; it feeds my heart and soul. It reminds me that I matter, I care enough to pay attention to what delights me, and I'm willing to invest extra energy to bring myself comfort and joy.

Hear

A varied compilation of sounds—music, voices, nature, noise, silence—empowers my presence.

I've been singing since the age of two and a half and played musical instruments for more than twelve years as a child, so music features prominently in feeding my sense of hearing. One of the things I discovered during my recovery was that when it came to music I had been starving my sense of hearing for years. When I became aware of accompanying my activities with music whenever possible and fitting the style of music to my specific activity, my general sense of well-being increased dramatically.

If the sounds of nature nurture you, make it a priority to spend time outdoors in all seasons. Find ways to bring the outdoors indoors. I love the sound of running water. I've incorporated that soothing sound into my home through two filtered water fountains for my cats. Those fountains support optimal physical health for my cats while feeding my sense of hearing. The one in my bedroom soothes me while I sleep. The one in my main living space helps me foster a sense of flow throughout my day. There are music players and files that feature a variety of environmental sounds to help bring the outdoors indoors if that is your auditory cup of tea.

I also found that I wasn't experiencing enough therapeutic silence. My professional consulting career was characterized by a noisy nonstop pace that left me feeling I never had a moment to myself and couldn't hear my own thoughts. During my recovery, I discovered the immense therapeutic value of intentional silence. I realized it was just as important to preclude overstimulating myself as it was to avoid understimulating myself.

Love, respect, curiosity, compassion, and gratitude are the hallmarks of my approach when it comes to balanced feeding of my sense of hearing as well. The goal is not to feel compelled to replicate what I do. It is to use what works for me as a key to unlock the secret of what might work for you.

Smell

An eclectic array of aromas—sweet, spicy, floral, fruity, earthy, pungent—seasons my journey.

When I began to be intentional about feeding all of my senses in a balanced way so that my sense of taste would stop leading me to fat- and sugar-laden foods in an attempt to fill sensory voids it could never hope to fill, I quickly shifted from being a sugar addict to being an aroma junkie. Based on the findings of *The Sense of Smell Lab* (2013), it's no wonder aroma proved such a compelling alternative:

> The sense of smell is thousands of times more sensitive than any of our other senses. In less than a millisecond, just one whiff of a familiar smell can trigger memories of childhood, home, and family.

Smell impulses travel faster than signals from sight or sound because the olfactory system is the only part of the brain that is directly exposed to the air.

The brain processes sensory information delivered through sight, sound, taste, and touch by identifying the incoming information first, which in turn generates an emotional reaction.

But our sense of smell is different. It does the opposite. The information of incoming odors is first processed by the emotions and subsequently identified. This places our sense of smell at the root of our emotional being.

Aromas delivered directly to the smell receptors in our brains have a powerful effect on behavior. Just think of your response to the smell of a cup of coffee in the morning or your reaction to a dead skunk on the side of the road.

Since birth, our smell receptors have catalogued every scent that passed through our nostrils in an area of the brain the size of a postage stamp. The average adult is able to process approximately 10,000 different smells, with each odor having the potential to evoke a memory.

Smell influences our moods, our emotions, and the choice of our mates. It is the main organ that contributes to our enjoyment of our sense of taste. Smells warn us of dangers such as fire, poisonous fumes, and spoiled food and give us awareness of our place in the environment.

Our sense of smell contributes enormously to the quality and enjoyment of our lives, our health, and our well-being. It is the mind-body interface.

The persuasive power of our sense of smell is the reason some realtors bake bread or cookies just before an open house. Your special treat may be the scent of fresh flowers, evergreen branches, or citrus potpourri.

Many people who now find themselves living alone for the first time in their lives confess that they get into a rut of not cooking real meals for themselves. They feel the preparation time just isn't worth the effort if it's only going to feed one person. Like everything else, if you don't cook because you don't enjoy it and would rather invest your time in other activities, then love is the core energy under your decision. But if you adore cooking and routinely produce fabulous, elaborate meals for guests but feel you are not worth more than a microwaved frozen dinner, it may be that fear is underneath your choice. Get curious; decide for yourself. Because you *do* matter; you are always worth the effort.

Yesterday morning I cooked a batch of homemade vegetarian chili in the crockpot. It smelled wonderful during the five hours that it bubbled away while I was preparing and broadcasting my weekly radio episode, enticing me with anticipation of the wonderful dinner to come. The aroma continued to linger for hours after I had put it all away in the refrigerator, greeting me each time I returned home after running errands. A gift that kept on giving by reminding me of the love I had demonstrated for myself by investing a little extra energy to prepare a home-cooked, healthy meal just for me alone. I matter. I am worth the effort.

Aromatherapy oils proved very beneficial. I found I didn't need to *eat* sugar cookies; I could be just as delighted by heating sugar cookie scented oils in my aroma burner. I became the queen of layering the same scent of shower gel, rich lotion, and eau de toilette on my body so the aroma lasted longer. I feed my passion for variety by switching styles every two weeks, rotating through sets that are sweet, savory, fruity, floral, spicy, and musky to keep my scent life interesting. The day Bath & Body Works came out with their limited edition iced cinnamon bun line of body care products, I was in ecstasy. So was everyone who encountered my sugar-and-cinnamon-drenched person. Total strangers, men and women alike, would stop me on the street and proclaim, "You smell fabulous! What is that scent?" Alas, in answer to your unasked question, that particular line is no more. But there are many other fruit- and food-scented options available in its place.

The same guidelines apply to sense of smell as the other outer senses. Be intentional; remember the findings of *The Sense of Smell Lab*. The scent of everything in your life matters: laundry soap and fabric softener, shampoo and conditioner, shower gel and bubble bath, dishwashing detergent and hand soap. Get curious and discover what works for you. Learning how to set and enhance your mood with scent is a skill you will be glad you developed. Calm, invigorated, sensual, or happy—there are aromas that can help you get there and stay there as long as you like. This applies especially to those of you who are highly sensitized and believe yourselves allergic to scent. Invest extra energy in figuring out what type and quantity of scent enhances your life. Your happiness matters. You are worth the effort.

Taste

A diverse mix of flavors—salty, sour, sweet, bitter, creamy, crunchy, juicy—adds zing to my days.

I left the sense of taste until last in this exploration of the outer senses for a reason. It's because so many of us gorge this sense with too much poor-quality food, hoping to distract ourselves or fill fear-shaped voids that overeating or consuming junk is never going to fill. By walking through the other four outer senses first, you are beginning to understand where and how you could better feed your senses of sight, touch, hearing, and smell instead of gorging your sense of taste.

If NASA employed superior design in building a state-of-the-art space vehicle and then cut corners by putting junk in the fuel tank, it wouldn't matter how sophisticated the engineering of the rocket: it would never reach its destination. So it is with human beings. You are a unique cocreative expression of the Divine here to do a big job: tuning in to the Universal frequency so you may channel love and light to reveal and advance the highest good for all, in all, through all. When it comes to food, it's not about deprivation and starvation. It's about creating the optimal rocket fuel for the rock star you are!

The key to achieving and maintaining balance in feeding my sense of taste, as with all of the outer and inner senses, is mindfulness in each moment. What's my objective? What's the optimal path? How am I doing? The five attributes of constructive core energy and all of the other inner and outer senses converge in the evaluation of each sense. Do my objective, path, and progress embody love, respect, curiosity, compassion, and gratitude? Am I employing all of the sensory tools at my disposal: a variety of nutrients, textures, colors, and scents? Is my presentation creative? Is my timing optimal? Am I demonstrating consistent commitment to my welfare by investing my energy in advanced planning, shopping, and preparation? Do I remain mindful and committed to fueling my sense of taste nutritiously at both ends of the emotional spectrum: celebration and disappointment?

There are scores of programs on nutrition and healthy eating. I was introduced to Weight Watchers in the 1980s when I wanted to lose ten pounds and they were using their original "exchange" structure. I had experienced anorexia in the 1970s and never wanted to go there again. Weight Watchers is not a fad diet for dropping pounds fast; it's a way of life, one based in mindful self-care, not deprivation. Its focus is to understand the principles of balanced nutrition, figure out where and why your relationship with food has gotten off track, and determine how to restructure your partnership to support you in being healthy and fit for life.

It's not about following the eating plan that worked for me. It's about mindfulness and self-love. Invest the energy to figure out what works best for you. I was a sugar addict, so I now avoid refined sugar wherever possible. While not hypoglycemic, based on my chemistry and makeup, I find my optimal approach is eating small meals every two to four hours that combine lean protein, whole grains, heart-healthy fats, and fresh fruit and vegetables. When we go too long without food, our bodies' primitive starvation monitors kick in and send the message to slow down metabolism for survival. It can take a while to get your rate of calorie burning back on track.

I discovered two additional reasons to drink lots of water, especially before and after meals. Sometimes when we think we're hungry, even though we ate a short while ago, we're actually dehydrated. This makes sense because our bodies use water to process our food. Try drinking a glass of water and see if the feeling you were tagging as hunger disappears. I also begin each day and each meal with a big glass of water with fresh lemon. It kick-starts the hydration, digestion, and fullness registration processes. One of the reasons we tend to overeat is because our bodies generally don't register "enough food" and turn off the appetite switch until about twenty minutes after we've eaten. Starting with water, eating at a reasonable pace, and paying more attention to nutritional quality and portion size than how full you feel are great habits to help you avoid overeating.

A couple of years after I gave up refined sugar in my food, I also gave up alcohol. It was the right decision for me. It is essentially concentrated sugar, so it sent me up and down the glycemic roller coaster and continued to feed the sugar addiction I was trying to be free of. For me, alcohol had insufficient nutritional value; it fueled mindless eating, slowed my metabolism, and had always been a depressant. Even one drink could produce depression that would still be evident the day after. Add to that a family history of alcoholism and, as a therapist once warned, for me, taking a drink was like putting a loaded gun in my mouth. Unsafe, unwise, and unnecessary.

I am not against alcohol or sugar or any particular food or drink. I am for mindfulness and self-love. I trust and respect you enough to know that, when fueled by love, you'll figure out what works best for you. Clear yourself of fear and trust your intuition. Once you are fueling yourself with constructive core energy based in love, respect, curiosity, compassion, and gratitude and you are feeding all of your senses in balance, you will find that what, when, and how much you eat falls into place just like everything else in your life.

As we bring this exploration of your sense of taste to a close, I'll share an interesting aside. I have found that in terms of the members on my personal board of directors, it's my muse, Bee, who has the greatest interest in food as a source of entertainment. When you learn more about the roles of the sage, guardian, and muse in chapter 6, the muse's perspective on, and potential obsession with, food will make greater sense. For now, just note that it is the muse who, if you are not feeding all of your senses in balanced ways, will sabotage the healthy eating process with junk food for the brief high it offers. Yet another reason to focus on feeding all of your senses if you wish to align your eating habits with optimal nutrition.

You matter. You are the only you we've got. Invest your energy in feeding your sense of taste optimally. You are worth the effort. There aren't enough cookies or french fries on the planet to smother anger, blame, shame, and self-loathing. Nothing you can eat or drink will fill a fear-shaped void. The good news is that nothing tastes as good as being healthy and fit feels.

Inner Senses—I Imbue My Experience with Meaning

Having made real progress by feeding my five outer senses, sixty pounds into my eighty-pound weight loss, I realized something was still missing. Reflecting more deeply on my own experience, I discovered, once again, greater insight and opportunity.

As magical as our five outer senses are in celebrating our world, to achieve genuine comprehensive sensory balance, we expand our perspective to include the four inner senses, with which *we imbue our experience with meaning.*

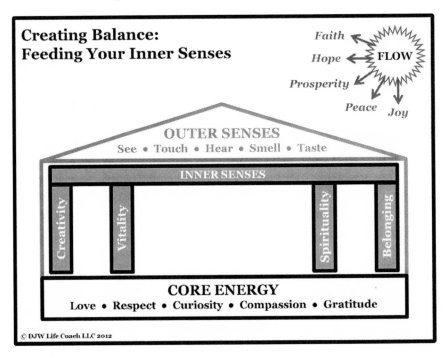

Figure 8: Inner Senses

Using the terms of the Discovery Framework, as the roof and outer walls of our energetic home, the outer senses are essential but will collapse if not supported by more than just our foundation of core energy. For long-term stability, they require the infrastructure and support of the four inner senses of creativity, vitality, spirituality, and belonging (figure 8).

Creativity

I imagine and manifest. I am passionate about new possibilities. I reveal and advance the highest good.

Julia Cameron's book *The Artist's Way* saved my life. My body, mind, and spirit began the Journey to Wholeness when I began living her teachings. I learned from Cameron that *all* of us are creative—not just those who call themselves Artists with a capital *A*. That our creativity is Divinely Sourced—as essential to sustaining life as oxygen, water, and food. Next time you are cranky or restless for no apparent reason, ask yourself the last time you did something that felt creative. If it has been more than twenty-four hours, there is a good chance *that* is the root of your discomfort.

We don't need to *learn* how to be *more* creative. We are *born* creative; it is our nature. We need to *learn* how to recognize and transform the layers of fear and limiting beliefs that block us from freely accessing and expressing all the creativity we already carry within us. We are creating in every moment in every area of our lives. It is a matter of what we choose to create. When I cling to fear and limiting beliefs, I create misery and lack for myself and everyone I encounter with everything I think, say, and do. When I choose to embrace love, with its attributes of respect, curiosity, compassion, and gratitude, everything I say and do creates a sense of generous, effortless, gracious flow filled with faith, hope, prosperity, peace, and joy for every being, encounter, and experience.

As Cameron shares in the February 17 entry of her daily readings book, *The Artist's Way Every Day—A Year of Creative Living,*

People frequently believe the creative life is grounded in fantasy. The more difficult truth is that creativity is grounded in reality, in the particular, the focused, the well observed or specifically imagined. As we lose our vagueness about our self, our values, our life situation, we become available to the moment. It is there, in the particular, that we contact the creative self. Until we experience the freedom of solitude, we cannot connect authentically. We may be enmeshed, but we are not encountered. Art lies in the moment of encounter: we meet our truth and we meet ourselves; we meet ourselves and we meet our self-expression. We become original because we become something specific: an origin from which work flows (2009).

To begin the search for my long-lost authentic self, I primed the pump with immersion in a plethora of creative endeavors. I had no master plan. Only a vague recollection of feeling happy just to be alive when I was making art as a child. Art is the language our souls still speak when our brains and mouths can no longer form words to tell our stories. Through our art, we self-disclose without ever planning to, even when we try not to. We can't stop our hearts and souls from speaking through our creations—whether we sing, garden, write, paint, cook, sew, repair cars, or fix computers. Always, and in all ways, we tell what longs to be told.

I found my authentic self three years into that search, living for the first time without other human beings in my home, and guided by love, respect, curiosity, compassion, and gratitude. Only then could I begin my first real connections with others. As Cameron observes, before that solitude, before that encounter with myself and my values, I was often, maybe always, enmeshed with others, but I never truly encountered them or they me.

Early in my experience as the Universal conduit for my blog posts, I learned the hard way never to force the writing on some arbitrary look-aren't-I-prolific timetable originated by my ego. Cameron advises repeatedly in her many books on the creative life that our egos should *never* be allowed to vote on anything we do—not if, what, how, when, how much, and most especially not on how effective we are at doing it.

One of the best ways to get our egos out of the way and relieve the pressure is to stop thinking of ourselves as the authors or originators of anything. We are the broadcast mechanisms for messages and inspiration from the Universe. Whatever our venue— writing, marketing, painting, architecture, quilting, legislature, musical composition, teaching, acting, child rearing, carpentry, singing—*we* don't create anything in isolation. We are cocreators with the Divine. Our primary responsibility is to stay tuned to the Universal frequency; be conscious of the inspiration and life lessons we are sent; remain courageous about sharing them; and do it with humility, compassion, a sense of humor, and a dash of rigor. Your life well lived is your greatest work of art. It will feed your soul and the souls of everyone you meet.

I've also learned that when the Universe shows up with something important to say, *do not ignore it.* Do not tell Her you just published yesterday and hadn't planned to write again today. Do not tell Her you have other priorities on your to-do list for today that you put off yesterday in response to Her call. Instead, respect Her wisdom on timing and topic, thank Her for continuing to consider you a worthy broadcast mechanism, and just do it. Don't be especially wedded to what *you* thought She wanted you to communicate. Stay in receptive mode as you go, because She may take you down a bend in the road to a totally different destination than you intended. Trust Her; She knows what She's doing.

My blog posting experience is a case in point. When I began, I published daily and then drifted to every few days, every few weeks, and finally months went by with no new posts. When I got curious about the decline in my rate of publishing, I realized it had little to do with busyness. Neither was it about having nothing to say or caring less about my readers. If anything, the reminders life had sent me concerning the fragility of our connection to people and things we hold precious had only deepened my compassion for all beings and taught me more that I wanted to share. What I discovered when I took a hard look at my relationship to publishing was that my *ego* was getting in the way. To address the situation, I decided I would find a way to make writing feel less monumental so that I would write more frequently, because connecting with humanity through my writing is an important way in which I realize my purpose on this earth.

One day, I got the bright idea to launch an additional blog (*Love and Curiosity: Gems for the Journey*) with the intention of publishing daily on that new site. My initial plan was to use the daily meditations from Julia Cameron's book *The Artist's Way Every Day* to create a very brief *Deborah-and-Julia* experience. I would expound briefly on one of Cameron's many inspiring thoughts, thereby passing the inspiration on to my readers with the possibility that they might choose to purchase Cameron's book and read it along with me. My plan was a lovely possibility for deeper connection with all humanity that warmed my soul. Cameron is an amazing writer. With Cameron providing guaranteed structure and inspiration, I would have tons of material to work with. Combined with the intentional brevity of my entries, I would leap gracefully over my writing resistance hurdle, publishing *Gems for the Journey* every day—no pain, no sweat. After all, I love writing and know I am an excellent writer. The day I found my voice again and began publishing the earliest content for this book online via my blog was a day of great gratitude and rejoicing for me. Now I had another cool idea for an easier and briefer blog. This should only multiply my publishing bliss, right?

Though my plan *seemed* brilliant, it neglected to consider one essential fact: it was my *ego* that was getting in the way of publishing with the regularity my heart desired. While this new plan was clever and mechanically sound—it could have produced the desired result—the reality is, it didn't. That is because it didn't do anything to deal with the very real issue of my *fragile* ego. Though the writing "assignments" were briefer, they were no easier.

Here are some of the many ways my ego showed up. First, my virtual best friend Cameron, the perpetually creative partner I was depending on for this escapade, totally let me down. I have read everything she has ever written. She has never failed to inspire *me* through *any* of her works. And yet she chose the day after I announced my new daily blog to become a lackluster writer. I would read her daily entry and say, "That's it? You expect me to inspire them with that? You had to pick now to become a lousy writer?" (Somewhere, I hope Cameron is laughing along with you and me.) Realizing that it was risky to depend so completely on such an obviously capricious genius, I decided I needed to include other inspiring teachers and writers if I was going to publish daily with ease. Thanks to input from that expanded team, I made it through a couple more posts.

Over the course of the six entries I published on the new site, I found that while all of my teachers inspired *me* on a daily basis, I still couldn't get that feeling out of my head onto the page. That, my friends, is because feelings don't come from our heads; they come from our hearts. I was reminded of this truth at the time by a session with my own life coach during which we were discussing my theoretical resistance to publishing, which I kept insisting was not a problem (*ha*). My coach observed that, in the first forty-five minutes of our sixty-minute session, each time she asked how I felt, I replied, "Intellectually, I think ..." Gotcha!

Like Jacob wrestling with the Old Testament angel, I wrestled with my ego every night. We managed to publish for five nights in a row with some difficulty but no big drama. It wasn't proving as easy as I'd expected, but I thought maybe I just needed time to get into a rhythm. Are you counting the number of times I've used *think, thought*, or a synonym? Big clue that I still didn't have a clue.

Which brings us to day six, Thursday, February 10, 2011. I awoke with many reasons to feel grateful for how my life was unfolding. Blessings continued to abound. Synchronicity without measure. Yet it was a harbinger of the day's events that I began with a "pep talk" from the fear-driven gremlin aspect of Ella, the guardian on my personal board of directors (more on guardians and gremlins in chapter 6). "Well, darling, 'love and curiosity' is a cute little writing effort. But it is clearly blog lite compared to your other site. Less taste and less filling. Less effort, less prose, less inspiring, just ... well ... less. I'll grant you that in some cases maybe less can be more (although I personally find that a lot more is always so much more). We both know if you would just buckle down and be a serious businesswoman again, you could do so much more with your life. Clients used to pay your consulting firms $750 for an hour of your insights. I find it so sad that this pitiful effort is what you've come to."

I recognized my fear-gripped arch nemesis, Cruel Ella (aka

Cruella) the moment she opened her mouth in my head. I told her to shut up, which she did. But remembering that she is really just part of me, I know that even when she doesn't make a sound, if she's afraid, that fear will be my undoing. It is no wonder I spent much of my day listening to Pema Chödrön lectures to counteract my gremlin's subliminal nagging.

The time of my blog writing got later every day of the first five days. Day six continued the pattern; I didn't sit down to write until 10:30 p.m. I was fresh off the exhilaration trail of listening to eight hours of Chödrön lecturing on meditation. She is brilliant, touching, and so very real. Her way of teaching meditative practice has helped me broaden and deepen my already eclectic and substantial spiritual practice. I even made notes during the day to make writing that night a breeze. I had ninety minutes in which to channel eight hours of Chödrön into three hundred to five hundred words that would transmit to all of humanity the essence of meditation and how meditative practice had transformed my life. A breeze? Not!

When the frustration level became unbearable, I considered ever more horrifying options such as just copying and pasting a few cool quotes from another site, declaring it a blog, checking off the daily box, and calling it a day. I began rendering that pitiful little solution right up to the step before pushing the "publish" button, when I pulled myself back from the brink in horror. Next I sat weighing the ethical ramifications of plagiarizing my own writing from my other blog site by pulling a clever paragraph from one of my previous posts there, pasting it onto the new site, signing it, calling it a blog, checking the daily box, and going to bed. No dice on that one either. At one point, I was so enraged with myself and the process that I considered obliterating the five existing entries and launching the site into blog oblivion (no issues with suppressed anger here). I stopped short of executing that one as well.

I know that whenever I create this much drama in my life, big lessons are in the wings. Stuff I need to pay attention to. The clock was running down. I had a little over sixty minutes before not publishing my daily blog that day would reveal me for the sham and lightweight writer I really was (so much for confidence in my writing abilities). All I had to do was convey the poignancy of Chödrön and the essence of meditation in three hundred words. How hard could that be? As it turned out, it was quite hard if I wanted to use only my head and not my heart to do it.

Because the resulting blog post is one of the most real and moving pieces I've ever written, I share it in the "Tonglen" section in the appendix of this book. Here is the lesson I relearned on that particular leg of my journey:

- I publish to touch others' lives. Sharing my vulnerability and growth inspires hope and courage within my readers and listeners.
- I don't have to publish lengthy pieces to touch lives. I write from my heart, not from a production schedule based on elapsed time and expected volume.
- I am the distribution channel, not the manufacturer, of my art. My role is to stay tuned to the Universal frequency of my endlessly creative Source and distribute what I am sent.

I close this exploration of your sense of creativity with an interesting client experience. Over the course of six months, my client had become committed to healthier eating and more-regular exercise with a personal trainer. While she had lost considerable pounds and inches at first, she quickly hit a plateau. Increased muscle mass wasn't the culprit. She tried being even more ambitious about calorie counting and exercise. No luck. During a coaching session, we did a quick scan to identify any sensory imbalances that might be at work. She realized she had been starving her sense of creativity for years. When she started feeding her creativity again, guess what happened? She started losing more pounds and inches. Without changing anything else about her calories or workout, she started losing more weight. Other clients have experienced similar successes once they started feeding their sense of creativity or other starved inner senses. Give it a try. What have you got to lose?

One of my theories about why this works is that, because we are complex, interconnected systems, our bodies register deprivation of any sense as starvation. They then shift into survival mode by slowing down the rate at which we burn the resources we still have at our disposal. As a result, our metabolism and rate of calorie burn slows to compensate. Conversely, when we stop starving any one of our senses, our bodies register satiation and our metabolism returns to normal. I can't prove this is why and how it works. I just know *that* it works. And *that's* good enough for me.

It has been said that God delights in expressing all aspects of Itself *through* us in cocreative partnership *with* us. In each moment, the question concerning creativity is, "Are you showing God a good time?" When was the last time you fed your creative inner spirit with no expected commercial outcome? Try something fun; borrow your kids' crayons, scribble a poem, organize your closet, paint a mural on your wall, sing a song, dance a jig, hit a bucket of golf balls, stick glitter stars on your ceiling, clean out your junk drawer, paint your toenails purple, just lie in the grass and dream as you watch the clouds go by. Your life *is* your greatest work of art. Expressing your unique self is why you are here.

Vitality

I thrive and inspire. I radiate stamina, strength, flexibility, stability, and dexterity. I am healthy, happy, and whole.

You may be expecting a section on exercise and fitness. When people ask what diet and exercise regimen I followed to lose eighty pounds, I tell them it's simple. Rebalance your calories in and calories out. Any questions?

The tricky part is how to do it so that it becomes a way of life, not a short-lived effort that lasts until your prom or fifty-year high school reunion. That's simple too. It starts by working on all the other aspects of the Discovery Framework because, as you know from reading my story, turning this way of living into a way of life was much more dependent on the mental, emotional, and spiritual changes, not just the physical ones. Here are some additional ideas to get the physical side moving in the right direction:

- Research and experiment until you identify nutritious, satisfying food you enjoy. I finally accepted that my relationship with refined sugar was an addiction. It may not be true for everyone, but it was definitely true for me. I went cold turkey on sugar and substituted fresh fruit and other complex carbohydrates.

- Research and experiment until you discover a form of exercise you actually enjoy. I got hooked on the mood-elevating effects of regular cardio at a brisk pace. I added in minimal strength training much later because I knew myself. In the past, weight work had fueled my appetite, and in the absence of a sustainable commitment to healthy nutrition, I had responded by consuming junk food with a vengeance. Cardio didn't have that side effect. This time, once my relationship with food had stabilized and I'd eliminated the foods I had an addictive relationship with, I could trust myself to add in strength training and increase my calories with healthy foods to support the additional workout. Maybe you enjoy the companionship and guidance of a personal trainer—one who will support you in your commitment to fun no-excuses baby-step goals so you don't end up an injured, burned-out exercise flash in the pan.

- Set initial improvement goals for nutrition and exercise that are so miniscule even you couldn't come up with a legitimate excuse for not achieving them. Maybe it is a reduction of one hundred daily calories and an addition of ten minutes of walking three times a week. Something so easy you are guaranteed to be celebrating success a week later.

- Continue small incremental increases to your goals whenever you feel inspired to do so. Don't ever push either goal to the point where you now have excuses for not meeting it. If you find you've pushed it too high, scale it back to the previous no-excuses level. Don't worry; slow and steady does work. Just ask the tortoise.

- Experiment with the optimal balance for quantity and type of calories and exercise until you have a sense of what works best to achieve your objectives.

- Make sure you are paying attention to rest and play, not just exercise and burning calories. It is all about balance, harmony, and understanding. Find ways to delight and feed your other senses while exercising: enjoy scenic vistas while walking, listen to audiobooks, or watch a favorite video. Then when you exercise, you won't think of it as work; you will think of it as stealing time to read a novel or watch the latest thriller.

In terms of setting your goals, an acronym from performance management consulting will serve you well. Learn to set SMART goals:

- **Specific:** What's the first baby step to move you in the direction of your goal? What will you do, how much of it, and how often? Which foods, what types of exercise, how many ounces, calories, and minutes?
- **Measurable:** For your initial baby step, how will you know you have succeeded? What will the quality or quantity of success look like? Inches or pounds lost, quality of calories consumed, minutes walking a certain distance. For what you have listed in the "specific" category, how have you qualified and quantified the measures of success?
- **Aligned:** Is your initial baby step and overall goal aligned with your core values? I find this one to be the hidden saboteur. Not just the values you admit to. For example, if you come from a family of chronically obese or out-of-shape people and one of your family values is that you always stick together, you might mistakenly conclude that getting fit would run contrary to that value. If you swear you want to accomplish something but you keep missing the mark, get curious. Ask yourself, "How might achieving this objective be out of alignment with a hidden value?" Then focus on the fear-based lies and illusions concealed in that value and set about transforming them and boosting your motivation by fueling it with a new love-based truth and reality.
- **Realistic:** Is this initial step really a no-excuses baby step? If you are a member of the club that always sets the bar inhumanely high, you may have a habit of sabotaging yourself right out of the gate. Make sure your goal is indeed a no-excuses baby step that is completely doable at this time in your life.
- **Time-Frame Anchored:** Make sure your specifics include exactly when you will complete your initial no-excuses baby step. For example, upon arising and before walking, you will consume a 250 calorie breakfast consisting of a sixteen-

ounce glass of water with lemon, one hardboiled egg, one ounce of string cheese, a slice of dry whole wheat toast, and a cup of black decaf coffee sweetened with stevia. Five minutes of walking every morning after breakfast and before you shower. Once this healthier way of living becomes a habit, you may find you can trust yourself to be more flexible about the timing. In the beginning, giving yourself structure helps support your success.

What to Do When You Fall Off the Wagon

Absolutely no beatings or self-berating. It will not help you do better in the future. It will demoralize you into giving up for all time. Remember the attributes of constructive core energy: love, respect, curiosity, compassion, and gratitude. Reread chapter 4. You will know what to do.

Why Such Minimal Goals Work

Read chapter 7 on tools for fostering flow, especially the "baby steps" and "celebrate" entries. Substantial, sustainable improvement of any sort is usually grounded in incremental improvement, not rapid leaps and bounds. Celebrate every step forward, no matter how small. If you exceed your no-excuses goal, that will result in even greater celebration. Force and extreme deprivation are not necessary. Excessive goals result in disenchantment, illness, injury, and burnout. Easy goals lead to easy success that fuels lasting motivation for a lifetime of even greater success.

For Perfectionists and Overachievers

In chapter 11 on finding a guide, I talk about the role I play in supporting clients with accountability. Here is an overview for your convenience.

I collaborate with clients to develop and implement a plan of action to move them closer to their hearts' desires. I support clients in achieving rapid, extraordinary, sustainable results by partnering and holding them accountable for what they commit to doing. In my experience, this takes one of two forms:

1. Helping those who have difficulty holding themselves accountable to learn to do so with love and respect by creating a reasonable plan based on a series of achievable baby steps that will allow them to flow into completion.

2. Helping those who've been accountable for everyone and everything since birth learn to eliminate much of what is on their list and, with love and respect, replace it with a reasonable plan based on a series of achievable baby steps that includes rest, reflection, and play at the top of the list. We can give nothing of lasting value from an empty well.

If you are in the latter group, then—having encouraged you to come up with a SMART plan for reaching your goals—I remind you that spontaneity is essential to a life of vitality. To illustrate the point, I will share two relevant examples from my own experience.

Example 1

The life cycle of my blog site is a great illustration of how overplanning and ridiculously high standards can drain the vitality out of an otherwise joyful experience. Still high on the thrill of having launched my first blog site on the spur of the moment with no exhaustive plan (not my norm), on Saturday morning three days later, I decided my plan going forward would be to write a new installment every day. Now that was more like the overachieving, pain-in-the-tukus Deborah my friends and family know and wish to strangle.

Let's take a wonderful, spontaneous event and turn it into an obligation. Let's suck every ounce of fun out of that puppy and make it a burden. Because heaven knows Deborah doesn't deserve to have fun. I mean, what would happen to the Universe if Deborah didn't have both hands on the steering wheel of life, keeping everything orderly and everyone safe? I kid you not when I admit that I had to use a thesaurus to find a word that means "unplanned" or "unrehearsed" (duh, *spontaneous*) for the first sentence of this paragraph. I knew there must be a word like that, and it kept flitting hither and yon in my head, but for the life of me, I couldn't grab onto it.

Why is it that spontaneity and I are such distant cousins? Because everyone knows that perfection is the only worthy goal in life and that perfection comes from planning, copious planning, nauseatingly exhaustive planning. Because planning controls destiny and keeps everyone safe, right? Not! Control is an illusion at best, and no amount of planning really controls anything. It organizes things and sometimes reduces the number of surprises, or the "surprisiness" of the surprises, but I firmly believe we do not *make* anything happen. If something is meant to be and you try to block it, it may take longer to manifest, but manifest it will. If it's not meant to be, no amount of planning or remaking yourself into what you think the situation requires will *make* it happen. It will just tie you up in knots and make you and everyone you know *cuh-ray-zee*! Witness the final eight years of my consulting career.

Lest you accuse me of advocating irresponsibility and sloth, I do think it's *useful* to plan. It's just important for us to realize that the Universe may not be in alignment with our plans. If that turns out to be the case, the sooner we recognize it and get ourselves in alignment with life's quirky, capricious, unpredictable plan, the happier we'll all be. If the events of the past five plus decades have taught me anything it's that despite my intelligence, intuition, and demonstrated anal retentive control freak planning skills, I sometimes don't have any idea what's best for me or anyone else. Thanks be to the Universe, which intervenes despite my best efforts to the contrary and forces Its plan on me whether I like it or not.

So back to my plan for my blog. Saturday I published two installments. Sunday I got busy with other things and missed a day. No problem. With two on Saturday, I was still on plan, I told myself, "averaging" one a day. Then Monday dawned bright and cheery. My plan for my day went like this: I'll have breakfast, do my written meditation, write blog posts for the rest of the morning, have lunch, go to the gym, study in the afternoon, have dinner, and create art in the evening. Tired yet?

In reality, it went nothing like that. I got up and made the mistake of looking at my email, and then I answered emails, paid bills, filed papers, ate a miniscule breakfast on the run, went to the gym, was exhausted when I finished because I had consumed insufficient calories to fuel my workout, went home, made a huge healthy raw veggie salad for lunch with two ounces of protein and an apple, and then proceeded not to eat most of it, opting instead to catch up on my sewing work because I'm a tester for an independent machine embroidery designer and I'd fallen behind in my sewing the week before while working on that thirty-three-page life review for my life coaching certification. Yes, I realize that was a long sentence. It was a long day.

Two new sewing clients showed up at 1:00 p.m. (I had neglected to account for their planned visit in *my* plan for the day) and stayed for an hour looking at designs, chatting, and playing with my youngest cat, Maisy Jane, putting me even further behind (how dare they have fun on my watch). I then sewed until 9:30 p.m., managing to multitask by planning a seven-part series for the blog on how I lost all the weight and refining my notes for my next twenty-three-page life coaching certification paper. At this time I realized I had consumed a total of 480 calories to fuel me during the first fifteen and a half hours of my day (*not* how I lost the eighty pounds last year and *not* my recommended diet). Then, because I had promised myself and everyone who cares about me that I wouldn't become anorexic as I did at age nineteen, I had to try to consume 1,500 more calories before bed. It's not an ideal way to balance daily caloric intake, but if some days I have to pack most of them into the final waking hour of the day, then by Jove, I do it. Anorexia is no joke.

Whenever people imply I have issues with control, I object. I have no issues with control. *I love it!* Unfortunately, it doesn't love me back. It's not even my friend. Most of the time it laughs behind my back, and sometimes it has the audacity to laugh right in my face.

So how does all of this fit in with the opening of this story? Given that Monday was a day when life and spontaneity conspired to laugh at my plan behind my back, I did *not* manage to publish the blog that day. Tuesday morning dawned cold and dreary. It was raining and forty degrees here in Colorado—a state that boasts three hundred sunny days a year and no humidity. I started the day by smacking myself around and insisting that today I would be much more disciplined—a synonym for *control*. (It's interesting that I know so many synonyms for *control* but so few for *spontaneous*). Clearly, I still didn't get it. So life and spontaneity had to team up yet again, filling my morning with things that needed to be done other than writing blog posts. I did have a few moments of enjoyment finalizing the materials order for a new art medium I was getting ready to teach, but otherwise I had no fun, I swear (like admitting to having fun would be a capital crime). Life and spontaneity tag-teamed me all morning. Six hours whizzed by. I had a minimal breakfast again, and I headed for lunch more than a little shaky, realizing I hadn't eaten much or written anything for the blog. I did some meditative breathing, which got rid of the symptoms but didn't address the root cause. So I said, "Fine. I'll just be a slacker again today, not write anything for the blog, and focus on my next life coaching paper for the rest of the day. Maybe I can finish the twenty-three-page paper in one day and then ..." You get the picture.

Unfortunately, I still wasn't getting the picture. There I was, driving to lunch, having given up my old plan, and working hard on my new plan, when in a moment of grace, it hit me: What if my plan *was* the problem? What if this was how I had given myself ulcers and anorexia by age nineteen? What if this was how I had become obese, burned out, and depressed at age fifty? What if my friend was right and it wouldn't matter where we worked? If we were stocking shelves in Target, we'd have to be the best darn shelf stockers Target had ever seen. What if, my dear friends, wherever we go, there we are?

Finally, the light dawned. I remembered what I knew in my soul: the world and I will be best served if I publish when I have something meaningful to say, not when I'm supposed to have something to say. That if my goal is to touch your hearts and save you some agony by sharing with you the often painful lessons I'm learning about how to have deeper peace, longer-lasting joy, and more meaningful relationships in my life, maybe the best way to do that is to stick to my end of the bargain. Pay attention to what is happening to me, figure out what it means, and pass on the message. I finally understood the difference between perfectionism and excellence. Perfectionism is not a lofty goal or enviable trait. *Perfectionism* is a fear-based illusion riddled with lies and characterized by force. *Excellence* is a love-based reality characterized by flow and grounded in the truth of who I am and Whose I am: a unique, cocreative expression of the Divine. The highest good—faith, hope, prosperity, peace, and joy—is not served by using force. The highest good is revealed and advanced through love, respect, curiosity, compassion, and gratitude.

Just like that, I was ready to write my next blog post. There I sat in a restaurant, without a plan, scratching notes on napkins and scraps of paper so I could hold onto all the insights until I could get back to my laptop to publish them.

My fellow travelers, I propose a much-needed holiday from all our planning. A day when we honor the gift of life by breathing with intention and feeling the blood coursing through our veins. A day when we just go with the flow, drink a leisurely cup of tea, read the paper, take a nap, play with the kids, pet the cat, and explore the possibilities. Because anything *is* possible. If I can baby step my way to deeper peace, lasting joy, and more-meaningful relationships, if I can finally get a life and not just make a living, then anyone can.

Example 2

Given that I had spent so many years confusing productivity with purpose, it's not surprising that five months later I needed another reminder concerning who I am and Whose I am and the fear-based nature of perfectionism.

Things had been humming along for me. Coaching six to ten clients a week. Publishing some, although not as much as I would have liked. Meditating, although more would have been beneficial. I had two assistants to help me catch up on office work and new technology to support greater efficiency. I was eating healthy, working out six days a week, and listening to good books on my PDA. I had an amazing online library system (www.librarything.com) to organize all of my favorite inspirational resources for clients. There was less clutter in the office. Making art was becoming a staple of my diet again. Sounds lovely, yes? *How could all of that abundance ever result in me weeping with my hands pressed over my heart?*

Here's my handle on the chain of events. I was cranking along, getting more organized and productive. Not realizing I was at risk for becoming seduced again by the gremlin of "productivity equals purpose" thanks to my guardian, Ella, falling out of love and into the grip of fear yet again. So at home was I in the land of overwork that I didn't even notice anything amiss when she started whispering and hissing in my ear, "See. Now you're remembering how this works. Work, work, work, and more work. Look at how much more you accomplish when you take yourself more seriously. Using those organizing tools again. Schedules, lists, software, how-to books. You used to raise multitasking to an art form. For heaven's sake, you taught others how to be more productive. I knew you couldn't have forgotten everything I taught you. All you needed was a little prodding from me. You know how much better it feels to be you when you're doing and accomplishing more."

I had no idea she had been playing that sinister tape in my head again. I knew my work could benefit from a little more intention and organization—setting priorities, making some lists, filing more regularly, scheduling more tightly. There is nothing wrong with being organized or productive. The problem arises when we conclude our value is in any way related to our performance. That is when things get wacky. It is when the other two members of my personal board of directors, my sage (Claire) and my muse (Bee), can be pulled out of alignment too, thanks to Cruel-Ella ruling with her iron fist of fear.

There I sat, sobbing and a bit clueless as to why. I had been up for hours and had consumed nothing but a cup of decaf cappuccino. I knew I needed to back away from the laptop, put some distance between my office and myself, go upstairs, and eat so my head and heart actually had some healthy fuel to function properly. Maybe add some sitting meditation to center myself and attain clarity. Upstairs to break the fast I went, beginning on-the-spot meditation by chanting my personal version of the Shambhala *Four Limitless Ones* affirmations, which are a way of life for me. At least I thought they were a way of life until I couldn't for the life of me remember one of the four.

I remembered the "peace" one because peace was so clearly eluding me at that moment. I had the "compassion" one, steeped in a misery of my own making as I was. I remembered the "joy" one, probably because I was experiencing none. What the heck was the fourth? I taxed my brain. I tried writing them down to trigger muscle memory. No dice. They had become the three, not four, *limited* affirmations. I had lost my way.

I knew in my heart it had to be significant that I couldn't remember the fourth. Maybe the root of my misery was that I quite literally couldn't remember and wasn't living the fourth. Unable to stand it any longer, I aborted breakfast prep and returned to my office to look up the fourth affirmation on my laptop. Here's what I found:

- **Love:** I enjoy loving-kindness and fostering loving-kindness.
- **Compassion:** I am free from misery and fostering misery.
- **Joy:** I choose joy.
- **Peace:** I dwell in equanimity, free from craving, aversion, and indifference.

Imagine my astonishment; the missing ingredient was love. *Love.* It's not the fourth; it's the first. How could I have forgotten about love? I am the love and curiosity chick. How had I forgotten about love, and how had it led to me weeping at the laptop? Simple. Deceived once again by the fear-based lie that productivity is the same as purpose, in the process of becoming more organized and productive I started to forget that the only reason to do so was to further my ability to always delight in my purpose to enjoy and foster loving-kindness. Not fussing and making myself crazy about having to be *perfect at it right now.* Not going nuts trying to figure out how I can read eight thousand self-improvement books this week to embody my purpose perfectly because *I'm not enough as I am.*

My sage, Claire, intervened: "Oh, Deborah, listen to yourself! Look at Little Bee. You're scaring her to death by pushing her way too hard again. Look at her. You've made her cry and hold her hands over her heart to protect herself from what you're doing to her. She's afraid she has no worth to you again because she's not perfect and can't do it all, doesn't want to do it all. She's worked hard for you all week. She had her heart set on playing some today. For love's sake, stop this insanity!"

Just like that, when I recalled that love *is* my purpose, I found the compassion, joy, and peace I had misplaced. I remembered that when I approach myself and every being, encounter, and experience with love, respect, curiosity, compassion, and gratitude, I always have deep peace, lasting joy, and meaningful relationships.

Dear ones, you are worthy just as you are, with your delightful blend of gifts and annoying little quirks. *In all of time, you are the only you in the entire Universe.* You are enough—perfect just as you are in *this* moment.

Spirituality

I believe and trust. My life is a purpose-filled journey, not a destination. I am more than I appear to be.

I repeat here a point I have made throughout this book: I provide specifics from my own life and experience. They serve as illustrations to inspire you to find your personal path to wholeness. My specifics are not prescriptions. Nowhere is that more true than when I share my thoughts on spirituality. To keep the writing simple and smooth, I will not preface every statement with the qualifier, "I believe." I respect all spiritual paths based in love, whether they use the word *God* or not. I benefit from all of them. Because you have chosen to read my book, I assume you are interested in knowing my particular perspective. Here goes!

Spirituality is about believing there is more to life than what we experience through our five outer senses. That there is more to everyone and everything than we are seeing, touching, hearing, smelling, and tasting in any given moment.

Spirituality and religion are not necessarily the same thing. For some people, participation in a form of organized religion is part of how they demonstrate their spirituality. For others, it's not. If you are one of those who carry painful memories of abuse you received in the name of religion, I invite you to free yourself from those painful memories now. Recognize that any damage inflicted was fueled by the perpetrator's fear. Spirituality is about love and endless possibilities; it is not about fear or lack. Choose love, embrace the possibilities of spirituality, and release with love and light any past pain you received in the name of religion. Please do not keep reinjuring yourself and limiting your world by continuing to rehash past injustices. Many who have let go of that painful past relationship with religion and have embraced a broader sense of loving spirituality have found their way home to a spiritual practice that better aligns with their definition of spirituality based in love.

God is not a four-letter word. Though some advisors warned me that using that word or its synonyms in this book might limit the marketability of my message, I have opted for authenticity. Please do not get hung up on a specific label. There are many names for this Force, because It is beyond words. I use a variety of labels: God,

Source, the Divine, Higher Power, Universe, Life Force, Creative Power, and Spirit, to name a few. The reality of God is so large, It transcends the limitations of any name or description I could conceive of. Substitute whatever label resonates most powerfully for you.

God is everywhere, within and without, always paying attention, always fully engaged with everyone and everything, and smart enough to know when whatever we're thinking or saying concerns Him/Her/It/Them. Thankfully, God is not dependent on us getting the words just right. God already knows it all. We are the ones who are figuring it out. Because God transcends time and space, nothing can limit Its power, including human constructs such as perceived barriers of language, belief, denomination, or spiritual institution. Though we sometimes elect to limit and separate ourselves through fear-based thinking, we are always one with everyone and everything, even when we choose not to remember or experience that good gift.

The great spiritual teachers did not come to earth as exceptions; they came as examples. They didn't come to say, "I'm It, and you're not." They came to say, "I'm It, and so are you!" They came to show us a larger way of being, what's possible when we free ourselves from fear and claim our birthright of love, creativity, wisdom, and power. Because God is love, there is no fear or scarcity when I remember that I am sourced in God. My Source is excellent, limitless, and reliable. I know *who* I am and *Whose* I am: a unique cocreative expression of the Divine. To honor them and because you may also find their teachings supportive on your journey, in the appendix of this book, I have included a selected list of the spiritual elders who have touched my life profoundly in recent years.

Prayer is not about begging God to care enough about me to help me or do it my way. God's full power and complete presence are available to each of us 24-7. A lack of interest on God's part is not the problem. Our fear-based limiting beliefs are the only blocks to living all of God's power and presence in each moment. Prayer and meditation are about being aware of when I have drifted off center, remembering *who* I am and *Whose I am*, realigning myself with the highest good, and recognizing where my chosen fear-based limiting beliefs are keeping me frightened, trapped, and small. It's about transforming that fear back into its Source Energy of limitless love and then expanding my presence to encompass all that is possible when I'm centered in that love.

A great spiritual teacher once said, "I have so much to do today, if I hope to accomplish everything on my list, I must meditate twice as long." In contrast, most of us are more inclined to say, "I have so much to do today, there's no way I have time for meditation or anything else!" I used to say that myself until I figured out that I have all the time I need for the things that matter. My only responsibility in each moment is to discern what matters most right now, to focus, and to follow through. People from spiritual traditions throughout the world have long reported that regular meditation results in greater efficiency, productivity, and prosperity. It amplifies the benefits of living in a state of generous, effortless, gracious flow grounded in who you are being *not* what you are doing.

Mindfulness and meditation are important elements in keeping myself centered and aligned with Source Energy. Paying attention and breathing. Any activity or lack of activity is meditative and restorative when I set an intention that it be so. Singing, walking, washing dishes, scooping cat litter, or doing absolutely nothing. While I sometimes engage in structured formal forms, meditation does not have to last for hours and involve uncomfortable postures to have a constructive effect. It just needs to happen, early and often. You will find a lengthier discussion of my thoughts on meditation in the appendix, including one of my favorite formal practices: written meditation, more commonly referred to as journaling. It also contains an overview of Deepak Chopra's free twenty-one-day meditation programs and a piece entitled, "Tonglen," which outlines a simplified form of Tonglen meditation.

While as a Reiki master teacher I sometimes offer Reiki treatments and programs that train and attune others in the practice of Reiki, my particular approach to living as a master is referred to as "walking the Reiki path." In that eclectic, intuitive, trans-denominational sacred space, everything I think, say, and do helps reveal and advance the highest good for all. For me, the "magic" is not in the tradition or symbols. The ability to facilitate physical, mental, emotional, and spiritual healing resides within each of us from birth. Invoking the Reiki symbols reminds me of the full range of God-given abilities that dwells within each of us at all times: *love, power, equanimity, healing, oneness, wisdom, manifestation, transcendence, and peace.*

When we are free of all fear and aligned with love as our Source, our very presence raises the constructive energy of every being and situation we encounter. In the appendix, I include the script for my personal affirmation-based daily practice with which I begin each day. Because I am a Reiki master, my practice includes affirmations based on the core intentions of the Reiki symbols. I share it to inspire you to develop your own personalized daily practice through which you clear yourself of all fear, realign your energy and intentions, and dedicate yourself as a clear channel for love and light, with the commitment to learn your lessons quickly and gently and help others do so as well.

In December 2010, after much study, reflection, and meditation, I chose to become an ordained minister. As a spiritual celebrant, I am licensed to officiate at civil and transdenominational spiritual services of all types. It is my particular honor to preside over celebrations of major life milestones and transitions such as birth, coming of age, graduation, relationship commitment, home blessing, healing, and end of life. Serving in this way is a natural complement to the partner, teacher, and guide roles I already embody as a life coach and Reiki master.

I was sent to be the unique Deborah Jane Wells cocreative expression of The Divine. I am not here to be an imitation of someone else. I am not here to fix you or turn you into an imitation of me. In the inimitable words of Oscar Wilde, "Be yourself. Everyone else is already taken."

This way of living is the antithesis of the kind of selfishness many of us were warned against in our youth. This way of living involves taking responsibility. When each person focuses on aligning herself with love, respect, curiosity, compassion, and gratitude, the world will exist in a state of generous, effortless, gracious flow filled with faith, hope, prosperity, peace, and joy for all. While that may be my *personal* vision and mission, I also know it is very possible. I know it because as a life coach and Reiki master I get to experience firsthand every day the dramatic transformation that unconditional love manifests in the lives of individuals who are becoming their own unique cocreative expressions of the Divine. When love transforms your relationship with yourself, *it can't help but transform your personal life, your work, and the world.* I know it. I see it. I live it.

When I remember *who* I am and *Whose I am* and focus my attention and intention on who I am *being,* what I think, feel, say, and do naturally aligns with the highest good. When I do not, it doesn't. Before birth in human form, when we existed as pure Spirit, we knew this. Part of deciding to take human form involved agreeing to forget this truth for a time so that we could experience remembering it again as we made our journeys back to the wholeness from whence we came. All of the wisdom and courage we seek is embedded deep within our Divine Essence. Every time we choose fear rather than love, we strengthen the barrier between what we know at our core and how we are choosing to show up. Years of fear-based living can produce a seemingly insurmountable impediment to accessing our truth.

You may be skeptical, "If she believes all of this, how did she end up morbidly obese with a decade of severe clinical depression?" The short answer is that, when I forgot what I knew, it took me a while to remember. Otherwise smart people are sometimes slow to embrace emotional and spiritual truths. I'm living proof that academic excellence combined with considerable drive, intellect, and creative gifts does not automatically produce wisdom. In my case, I believe all that ability and accomplishment may have proven one of my greatest barriers. While I always believed that my gifts were Divinely Sourced and I had a robust spiritual practice for many years of my life, *I still thought I was making it all happen and, most destructive of all, that my worthiness was based on the quality of my productivity and performance.* When I finally encountered an external standard I could not figure out and could not meet no matter how hard I tried, it nearly destroyed me.

Being an overachiever, I tried overdoing a variety of things in a vain attempt to numb myself from the pain of failure and distract myself a while longer from finding the truth, which is that each of us are Divinely Sourced in love and therefore utterly and completely worthy in every moment no matter what we believe or how we're performing. Many of the world's great spiritual traditions share this same essential truth in a variety of ways: the Kingdom of Heaven is within.

I overworked—no vacations for years at a time. I overdid shopping, eating, drinking, and talking. I proved especially adept at overcollecting all manner of objects, my most impressive being a collection of more than two thousand Barbie dolls, complete with twenty different fully outfitted doll dwellings. That particular example was a failed attempt to recapture joy by re-engaging in a joy-filled aspect of my childhood. Because I needed to find some joy, I needed it desperately. By the time I donated my beloved Barbies and all my other collections to charities for auctions, I was hanging on to life by the skin of my teeth. My major challenge each day was to find a reason to go on living.

Sometimes, when we get stuck in habit, ego, or despair, we need to be worn down and broken open to get it. Fortunately, the Universe is more wise, creative, persistent, and loyal than I am, even on my best day. When I didn't rediscover my truth via the first one million transmissions, the Universe didn't give up on me. It just upped Its game and kept right on transmitting until I was finally ready to listen, remember, and respond with clarity concerning why I am here and how I choose to live.

To help me gain greater clarity concerning what it means when I affirm that I know *who* I am and *Whose* I am, I developed a highly personal statement of intentions based on my values and purpose. I share it in the appendix to inspire you to become clear and intentional about your own precious life based on *your* values and purpose. My statement is posted over my desk, in my kitchen, and next to the bathroom mirror—places where I tend to linger over tasks and benefit from the opportunity to remind myself of my core beliefs and motivations. In particularly stressful situations, I recite a relevant item from the list. Other times I read the entire list aloud as an overall reminder. I encourage you to experiment with developing your own deeply meaningful intentions and ways of using them to support you on your Journey to Wholeness.

Belonging

I connect and communicate. I enjoy meaning-filled relationships with myself and others. I know and am known.

Healthy boundaries are not about separation; they are about creating an environment that fosters constructive core energy. One of the greatest gifts we give others is not choosing to love them; it is having the generosity and courage to allow them to love us.

If at this point in our exploration you're hoping for a big dose of holding hands and singing "We Are the World," you're in for a disappointment. Relationships are not for the naïve or faint of heart. There's a reason I cover this inner sense last. Relationships are the doctoral program of life lessons. Just when we think we're starting to get the hang of living from unconditional self-love, the Universe raises the bar and sends us relationships. As challenging as you may have found this path so far, self-love is by comparison relatively easy to accomplish in isolation. It is much trickier in community with others.

Relationships offer the opportunity to recognize and transform any and all vestiges of unexamined fear within ourselves, thereby becoming even clearer channels for love and light at all times and in all situations. They are, in the words of George Frideric Handel's *Messiah*, "the refiner's fire."

Intimate relationships are loving mirrors. The adage of opposites attracting is based in part on the idea that we seek in our companions a way to complete the underdeveloped or unappreciated parts of ourselves. Now *there* is a formula for friction! You can choose to walk around feeling annoyed and put upon most of the time or, like the oyster, choose to embrace the irritant and set your intention to create a pearl. It's up to you. You are the decider; what will you do with your precious gift of life? How might you find greater joy in your relationships if you weren't so attached to tolerating them with resentment?

Kick all thoughts of "fixing" others to the curb. Even if they let you do it, it is not kind. It robs them of their personal power and opportunity for personal growth. By forcing a situation on them that they may not be ready for, you expose them to a sense of failure and cheat them of the opportunity for authentic, organic growth that could have empowered them by unfolding in its perfect time. As with the man who thought he was making it easier for the struggling butterfly by cutting it out of the cocoon, it does not matter what you *think* your motivations are; the butterfly is still dead, and you're the one holding the scissors. It is neither respectful nor realistic. You can't *make* anyone change. Substantive, lasting change comes from within.

Share ideas and possibilities freely. Then completely detach from the outcome. When you find it hard to do so, your real opportunity is not to "fix" the other person's life. It is to figure out what feeling you believe you'll have, the one you won't let yourself have now, once they get in alignment with your plan. Next, get curious about what fear is blocking you from allowing yourself to feel that feeling, just as things are. Finally, determine what truth and love-based reality you could substitute for your chosen fear-based lie and illusion to produce the desired feeling for yourself right now, without *anyone else* having to change *anything else*. If you are really interested in changing someone's life for the better, focus on the only life for which you have been given both the responsibility and ability—your own. In the process, you will find that moods can be contagious. Your greater joy and fulfillment will improve the experience and opportunities of everyone and everything you encounter.

What kind of companion are you, and what type of people do you spend most of your time with? Honest, optimistic, encouraging people committed to mutual growth? Companions who share deep, meaning-filled relationships? People who lift one another up and help raise one another's energetic frequencies when they are low? Or wet blankets, devil's advocates, and downers?

Take great care in choosing your closest relationships. While we may have great love, respect, and compassion for others who are choosing to fuel themselves with fear, it is not necessarily optimal to expose ourselves to a constant diet of such companions. Yes, mindfulness can help you keep yourself clear, but a constant need to be on alert for attitude and mood contagion is exhausting. While challenging relationships present great learning opportunities, they are debilitating on a regular basis. Even the strongest among us needs a break now and then. Pay attention to what you are feeding your sense of belonging.

One of the reasons we become stuck in codependent, mutually

destructive relationships is that we are resisting appropriate allocation of responsibility. When we choose to remain attached to the energy of regret and resentment, we entrap ourselves in a shame and blame web of our own making, unable to break free into self-responsibility and healthy detachment. Learning to bring to bear unconditional love, respect, curiosity, compassion, and gratitude produces the shift from a disempowering core energy of fear, reeking of "I don't matter" and "I am powerless," to an empowering core energy of love, emanating "I matter" and "I am powerful."

Relationships have been the greatest teachers in my life. While often they didn't feel helpful at the time, in hindsight I can see that they provided the sacred space in which I received my most difficult lessons about the true meaning of healthy boundaries. They were the classroom in which I learned how to establish constructive limits for myself and how to recognize when my "desire to help" was not fueled by core energy of love but by fear in the form of anxiety, self-doubt, avoidance, or arrogance.

Across a variety of roles and venues—daughter, sister, parent, wife, mother, boss, subordinate, coach, friend—I had to be taught these lessons about respecting my own and others' boundaries again and again before I began to see the light. These same advanced classes are the ones to which the Universe continues to invite me each day.

Don't set your intention to develop more patience or better boundaries unless you are prepared to embrace the inevitable upheaval. We only become better at anything with practice. Practicing patience and boundaries requires doing so in difficult situations. It is the only way to get good at it.

I'll share a few personal examples to illustrate. In the introduction to the Discovery Framework, I mentioned a couple of belonging-related hiccups I encountered on my way to writing this section of the book. These situations provided the latest in a series of ongoing moment-by-moment opportunities to deepen my own ability to live the framework, clarify my boundaries, and strengthen my commitment to my calling. They included two of my beloved cats being diagnosed with illnesses; my husband undergoing two surgeries in one month, with two more to come; and a rift in a long-term friendship.

So how did I fair? I remained on an even keel in handling the two cat-astrophes, demonstrating real progress in my ability to be fully present when I perceive my loved ones are in pain or danger. I didn't even consider my past practice of spinning death horror stories in my head that would only serve to freak me out and block me from accessing my deepest wisdom. I embraced my responsibility for my cats' diagnoses and care and continued chipping away at sculpting the framework chapters of this book. I remembered that all relationships are sent to us for a season and a reason. I practiced being here now, appreciating every moment life gives me with the furry family members I adore.

I also did fairly well with my husband's surgeries, trying to be supportive (love) without being intrusive (fear). I freely admit to a few times when I stuck my nose in and pushed my approach over his (disrespect). The good news is that I noticed my slips quickly (curiosity), didn't beat myself up (love, respect, and compassion), apologized voluntarily (love and respect), and shifted my focus back to writing the framework chapters, trusting Wilson to manage his own healthcare.

The rift in the friendship proved the greatest challenge of the three for me. I did a bit of obsessing, which distracted and blocked me from writing and other happy endeavors. But I also handled it, especially the fear, much more constructively than I have such situations in the past. I applied curiosity instead of judgment in assessing what my friend and I each contributed to the rift. Over a period of months, I made multiple attempts to repair it. When it became clear to me that reconciliation was not in the cards, I released all of it with love and light and firmly but lovingly closed the door. For me to have pushed the situation any further at the time would not have been loving, respectful, or compassionate to either of us.

With deep disappointments, this release process is often iterative. When the pain of such experiences resurfaces periodically, I try to resist distracting myself with eating to excess, shopping until I drop, or working harder and longer. I set my intention to embrace my feelings with curiosity and identify the opportunity for even deeper healing within me. Sometimes there's an aspect for which I bear responsibility that I've not fully accepted. Other times there's an element of my friend's responsibility that I'm still trying to carry.

I focus my energy on embracing my own lessons and completely detaching from my friend's lessons because, frankly, they are none of my business. I have enough on my own plate at all times to keep me constructively occupied. I remind myself that we each did the best we could with the wisdom we gave ourselves access to at the time. I foster genuine gratitude for the growth our relationship has offered me and release both of us into the loving arms of the Universe to move forward on our individual paths.

I am genuinely grateful for the advanced class in boundary setting and the opportunity to share it here (yet another silver lining). In the Bible, Ecclesiastes 3:1 (*The Message* version) tells us, "... there is a right time to everything on earth." The Tao rules of engagement for right relationships express this principle as, "When you come, we welcome you. When you stay, we do not hold on to you. When you leave, we do not pursue you."

If the Universe feels my friend and I still have unfinished business, It will reopen the door when the time is right. If not, the time may have come for us to move on permanently because we are meant to learn our remaining life lessons through other situations and relationships. One way or another, we're going to keep being offered the lessons until we learn them. The longer it takes, the tougher the lessons get. As we say in the practice of Reiki, "May I learn my lessons quickly and gently and help others do so as well."

Sensory Balance Scan

Now that you have greater insight into the importance of feeding all nine of your senses in balanced ways, you are better equipped to notice when any one of them would benefit from recalibration and what form that might take.

While it is possible to gorge or starve any of our senses, because sacrificing food *quality* while overdoing food *quantity* is a nearly universal experience, I will use it here to illustrate the spirit of my approach. One of the great benefits of embracing rather than ignoring or denying my habit of using food to fill un-food needs is that I now have an incredibly reliable barometer for when something is out of alignment within me.

My agreement with myself regarding eating is that I pay attention to the quality and quantity of what I am ingesting. If I find myself overeating, even healthy fare, when I know I shouldn't be physically hungry, my promise is that I respect myself enough to be honest about what's really going on. I stop and run a quick scan to see if I can determine what may be troubling me or where my life has gotten out of whack. What sense other than taste might I be starving that I'm trying to compensate for by overeating?

I also look for any evidence of the nutritional equivalent of plopping my child in front of the TV to avoid giving her my undivided attention. What strong emotion might I be avoiding by distracting, titillating, and lethargizing myself with excessive poor-quality food?

Whether you are overeating, overworking, or overshopping, the essence of the sensory balance scan is this: I love myself enough to pay attention. I respect myself enough to be honest about what's really going on. I am curious about whether what I am doing will really help or, in fact, if it will just injure me further. I have compassion for whatever I find, and a commitment to be more supportive. I am grateful for the deeper insights and additional opportunities for growth.

Sensory Balance Scan

When I feed all of my senses in a balanced way,
no one sense takes over trying to fill a void it can never hope to fill.

		Starve		Just Right		Gorge	Baby Steps to Improve Balance
Outer Senses: I celebrate my world.	See						
	Touch						
	Hear						
	Smell						
	Taste						
Inner Senses: I imbue my experience with meaning.	Creativity						
	Vitality						
	Spirituality						
	Community						

INSIGHTS:

© DJW Life Coach LLC 2012

Figure 9: Sensory Balance Scan

Figure 9 provides a simple form to guide this process. As with the flow and core energy scans, the sensory balance scan consists of five steps, with each step grounded in caring enough about yourself to do the following:

- Pay attention so that you notice quickly whenever you've drifted into a state of sensory imbalance due to starving and/or gorging one or more of your nine senses. Realize that gorging one or more of your senses is likely to indicate starving one or more and vice versa.
- Invest your energy in assessing the root cause of the imbalance, paying special attention to any fear underneath what you are thinking, feeling, saying, and doing.
- Determine what baby steps will strengthen the presence of love in your reality and restore balance to the way you are feeding your senses: quality, quantity, and frequency.
- Hold yourself accountable for following through on your commitment to take action.
- Assess your results and continuously refine and expand your action plan to maximize the presence of love and minimize the presence of fear, thereby restoring harmony and encouraging sensory balance.

Having gotten honest with myself, if the results of the scan indicate there is something significant to explore but I don't yet feel able to go deeper, I demonstrate respect and compassion by not forcing myself. If I still feel that distracting myself with food is the best I can do with the love and light I have at the time, then I may go ahead and eat five pounds of raw vegetables. But I will have planted the seed and taken an additional step in recognizing unresolved fear inside me, moving myself forward on my personal Journey to Wholeness.

For more insights into creativity and sensory balance, read *The Artist's Way* by Julia Cameron.

Chapter 6:
Achieving Equanimity—
Your Personal Board
of Directors

You may say, "So far, the principles sound great in theory, but you've neglected to take into account the oppressive power of the judgmental voice in my head. Every time I start to break free from thoughts of self-imposed limitation and lack, that voice puts me back in my place by reminding me that I'm not good enough and never will be." Good news! Help is on the way. Once you build a more constructive relationship with your personal board of directors—sage, guardian, and muse—you will find that disparaging voice becomes less prevalent *and* less powerful (figure 10).

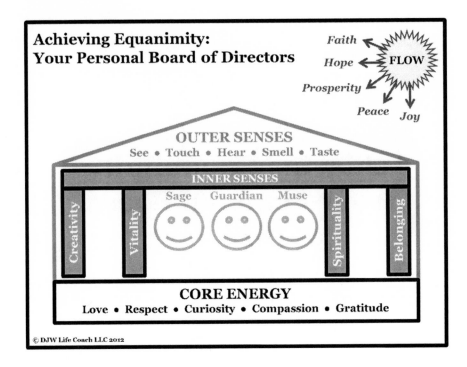

Figure 10: Your Personal Board of Directors

When your board members collaborate respectfully, they leverage their vast collection of competencies, seamlessly drawing on your constructive core energy and feeding all of your senses in a balanced way. When fueled by love, your board members are capable of synthesizing their diverse strengths and talents into a whole that is much greater than the sum of its parts.

When your board is working smoothly and constructively, as they were when you arrived in this world, they function much like a single-lever water faucet that seamlessly mixes hot and cold water to the optimal temperature for a variety of purposes.

When your board members are fueled by love, you can trust their discernment—*reasoning and intuition*—to help you foster equanimity and access your deepest wisdom to reveal and advance the highest good for all, in all, through all. They do this by creating a moment-by-moment custom blend of competencies that varies based on the optimal mix for the opportunities in each life situation.

I am reminded of the teaching I heard from Deepak Chopra:

EGO stands for "edging God out." Based on the laws of algebra, if EGO equals edging God out and God equals love, then EGO equals edging *love* out. That's precisely what happens when your board members become dysfunctional. When they switch to fear as their fuel instead of love, they block your forward progress by focusing their energies on infighting, backbiting, and one-upmanship on a grand scale. In short, they keep you small because they believe that is what safe looks like. The answer is for you to get to know each of them intimately and coach them into a more expansive, love-fueled approach to life.

Awareness of your board of directors is not an indication that you have multiple personality disorder. The construct of a personal board is a useful device. Sorting your vast array of gifts, passions, options, fears, and coping mechanisms into three distinct though interrelated subsets reduces the complexity of understanding what's going on in each moment and the specific path to finding greater equanimity.

A reminder: whatever pronoun is used, assume gender neutrality in all descriptions. It makes for smoother reading just to vary the use of masculine, feminine, and neutral pronouns than to constantly indicate female and male in every instance. While it is true that an individual board member may show up as primarily male or female, such designation refers to the member's energetic signature, not its anatomic gender. Your board members may all be male, all female, all androgynous, or any combination thereof.

Your Board Members' Agendas

Each member of your personal board of directors has its own agenda and unique set of core competencies. The elements of those agendas are shown in figure 11 and include the following:

Your Board Members' Agendas
The whole is greater than the sum of its parts.

MEMBER: *Focus*	SAGE: *Soul*		GUARDIAN: *Head*		MUSE: *Heart*	
Love Persona	Optimist		Engineer		Visionary	
CORE FEAR	I DON'T MATTER				I AM POWERLESS	
ATTRIBUTES	LOVE-BASED	FEARS	LOVE-BASED	FEARS	LOVE-BASED	FEARS
• Goal	Meaning	Nihilism	Safety	Danger	Fun	Drudgery
• Means	Synergy	Discord	Structure	Chaos	Flexibility	Constraint
• Gift	Discernment	Confusion	Discipline	Laziness	Imagination	Monotony
• Passion	Flow	Force	Work	Waste	Play	Servitude
Fear Persona (GREMLIN)	Bleeding Heart Hermit Know-It-All Zealot		Killjoy Workaholic Drill Sergeant Control Freak		Dilettante Sneak Wild Child Loose Cannon	
Defense Mechanism	Withdrawal and Annihilation		Condescension and Coercion		Deceit and Rebellion	
Remedy	See the Opportunity		Make a Plan		Find the Fun	

© DJW Life Coach LLC 2012

Figure 11: Your Board Members' Agendas

- **Focus:** Where each places its primary attention.
- **Love Persona:** Their optimal constructive way of showing up when fueled by love.
- **Core Fear:** Their lowest common denominator shared fear. This core fear leads each of them to forget the truth of a reality based in love and oneness and choose instead to become victims to the lie of an illusion based in fear and a sense of separation.
- **Attributes:** Their primary love-based qualities and specific fears that can undermine those qualities, including their
  - **Goal:** Utmost desire;
  - **Means:** Preferred way of fulfilling their goal;
  - **Gift:** Greatest natural aptitude and most valuable contribution to every situation; and
  - **Passion:** Chief delight, what brings them the most joy in life.
- **Fear Persona:** Their most common destructive ways of showing up when fueled by fear, also known as their gremlin personas or "going gremlin."

- **Defense Mechanism:** Their favorite passive and aggressive forms of sabotaging you. Typically, they begin to assuage their fear by using passive aggressive techniques to dissuade you from your chosen path. If those prove ineffective, as their fear continues to grow, they usually switch to more aggressive tactics.
- **Remedy:** The nature of the first baby step that will begin to lead them out of their fear-based, sabotaging gremlin persona and restore them to love and a sense of oneness.

Sage's Agenda

The sage's agenda and core competencies are summarized in figure 12. The sage places its primary attention on matters of the soul. When its core energy is fueled by love, it shows up as the eternal optimist: everything's an opportunity to the sage centered in love. When the sage forgets the truth of a reality based in love and oneness and chooses instead to become a victim to the lie of an illusion based in fear and a sense of separation, its core fear is the same two-part core fear of your other personal board members: I don't matter; I am powerless.

Sage's Agenda

MEMBER: *Focus*	SAGE: *Soul*	
Love Persona	Optimist	
CORE FEAR	I DON'T MATTER I AM POWERLESS	
ATTRIBUTES	LOVE-BASED	FEARS
• Goal	Meaning	Nihilism
• Means	Synergy	Discord
• Gift	Discernment	Confusion
• Passion	Flow	Force
Fear Persona (GREMLIN)	Bleeding Heart Hermit Know-It-All Zealot	
Defense Mechanism	Withdrawal and Annihilation	
Remedy	See the Opportunity	

© DJW Life Coach LLC 2012

Figure 12: Sage's Agenda

The specifics of how that core fear manifests for the sage are aligned with the sage's love-based qualities and attributes. Its goal, or utmost desire, is finding meaning and believing that everything has a constructive purpose. The specific fear that challenges that desire is nihilism: the possibility that anything—or worse yet, everything—is random and meaningless. The sage is especially susceptible to pessimism and despair.

The sage's means, or preferred way of fulfilling its desire for meaning, is synergy, believing that maximizing collaboration always enhances everyone and everything. The specific fear that can test the sage's belief in the universality of a synergistic path to meaning is discord: any form of conflict, friction, or arguing.

The sage's gift, greatest natural aptitude, and most valuable contribution to every situation is discernment. The specific fear that undercuts the sage's ability to demonstrate and contribute discernment is confusion of any sort: bewilderment, disorientation, or upheaval.

The sage's passion and chief delight—what brings the sage the most joy in life—is a sense of flow: a generous, effortless, gracious way of being. The specific fear that thwarts the sage's passion for flow is any feeling of force: pressure, coercion, or bullying.

When any or all of the sage's specific fears awaken the core fear that the sage does not matter or is powerless, it stops showing up as the eternal optimist. Instead, it takes on one of its many gremlin personas, including the bleeding heart, hermit, know-it-all, or zealot.

The sage's initial passive aggressive technique to dissuade you from your chosen path is often a form of withdrawal. Denial and depression are the tools of the frustrated sage. The bleeding heart and hermit personas are most common in this stage. When passive aggressive techniques prove ineffective, as the fear continues to grow, the sage will switch to more aggressive tactics of annihilation: elimination of itself in the form of suicide (figurative or literal) or elimination of others through ruthlessness and murder (figurative or literal). The fear is so unbearable that the sage will do anything to make it stop, including employing force-based tactics that are antithetical and horrifying to its normal passion for flow. The gremlin personas of the know-it-all and zealot are common in this stage.

There is a simple remedy for breaking this self-destructive cycle, leading the sage out of its fear-based, sabotaging gremlin personas and restoring it to love and a sense of oneness. The key is to help the sage *see the opportunity*. Just a small glimmer of a possibility buried under all the fear and then the first baby step in the direction of manifesting that possibility is all it will take. Opportunity is the medium in which the sage thrives. Opportunity will cause the sage's natural aptitudes and abilities to return, strengthen, and grow. When that happens, harmony and synergy with your other board members will be restored.

Whenever you start to feel pessimistic or melancholy, be alert for the possibility that your sage is shifting into gremlin mode due to fear. The equanimity scan in figure 15 can help you diagnose the root cause and return your sage to its more constructive persona.

One of the interesting and challenging realities is that once one board member becomes aligned with fear, the nature of the passive and aggressive tactics to which it defaults will increase the likelihood that one or both of your other board members will be pulled out of alignment in reaction to the first member's antics. For this reason, it is especially important to form deep, intimate relationships with each board member and pay attention to the earliest warning signs that something may be amiss. A sage not quickly restored to love will result potentially in a much more complex task of working to restore two or more members with very different agendas at the same time.

When life feels like it's running amok and gremlin voices are the only ones you hear, it is quite common to find that each of your board members has become afraid of different aspects of the same situation. It is possible to work with all of them at the same time by addressing each patiently and individually based on their particular orientations. It's just more advanced work. It is much easier to always stay tuned to their distinct frequencies and address any fear-based anomalies in their perceptions before they grow to mammoth proportions.

Guardian's Agenda

The guardian's agenda and core competencies are summarized in figure 13. The guardian places its primary attention on matters of the head. When its core energy is fueled by love, it shows up as the chief engineer: everything is a puzzle to be solved to the guardian centered in love. When the guardian forgets the truth of a reality based in love and oneness and chooses instead to become a victim to the lie of an illusion based in fear and a sense of separation, its core fear is the same two-part core fear of your other personal board members: I don't matter; I am powerless.

Guardian's Agenda

MEMBER: *Focus*	GUARDIAN: *Head*	
Love Persona	Engineer	
CORE FEAR	I DON'T MATTER I AM POWERLESS	
ATTRIBUTES	LOVE-BASED	FEARS
• Goal	Safety	Danger
• Means	Structure	Chaos
• Gift	Discipline	Laziness
• Passion	Work	Waste
Fear Persona (GREMLIN)	Killjoy Workaholic Drill Sergeant Control Freak	
Defense Mechanism	Condescension and Coercion	
Remedy	Make a Plan	

Figure 13: Guardian's Agenda

The specifics of how that core fear manifests for the guardian are aligned with the guardian's love-based qualities and attributes. Its goal, or utmost desire, is finding safety and believing there is no risk of harm. The specific fear that challenges that desire is danger: the possibility that anything—or worse yet, everything—is a threat. The guardian is especially susceptible to overreacting by seeing every instance of the unexpected as a harbinger of jeopardy or peril.

The guardian's means, or preferred way of fulfilling its desire for safety, is structure, believing that maximizing order, specificity, and predictability always enhances everyone and everything. The specific fear that can test the guardian's belief in the power of structure to ensure safety is chaos: any form of unruliness, pandemonium, or anarchy.

The guardian's gift, greatest natural aptitude, and most valuable contribution to every situation is discipline. The specific fear that undercuts the guardian's ability to demonstrate and contribute discipline is laziness of any sort: lethargy, sloth, or inertia.

The guardian's passion and chief delight—what brings the guardian the most joy in life—is a sense of work: quality and productivity. The specific fear that thwarts the guardian's passion for work is any feeling of waste: carelessness, extravagance, or redundancy.

When any or all of the guardian's specific fears awaken the core fear that the guardian does not matter or is powerless, it stops showing up as the chief engineer. Instead, it takes on one of its many gremlin personas, including the killjoy, workaholic, drill sergeant, or control freak.

The guardian's initial passive aggressive technique to dissuade you from your chosen path is often a form of condescension. Sarcasm and superiority are the tools of the frustrated guardian. The killjoy and workaholic personas are most common in this stage. When passive aggressive techniques prove ineffective, as the fear continues to grow, the guardian will switch to more aggressive tactics of coercion: brute force to remove any perceived barriers to safety. The fear is so unbearable that the guardian will do anything to make it stop, including bullying and screaming that are antithetical and horrifying to its cool-headed, analytical norm. The gremlin personas of the drill sergeant and control freak are common in this stage.

There is a simple remedy for breaking this self-destructive cycle, leading the guardian out of its fear-based, sabotaging gremlin persona and restoring it to love and a sense of oneness. The key is to help the guardian *make a plan*. Not a fear-based three-thousand-item fifty-year plan in twelve-hour increments. Just a small suggestion of a path out of the chaos and then the first baby step in the right direction. Await feedback from the Universe and then take the next baby step. Planning is the medium in which the guardian thrives. Planning will cause the guardian's natural aptitudes and abilities to return, strengthen, and grow. When that happens, harmony and synergy with your other board members will be restored.

Whenever you start to feel rushed or tense, be alert for the possibility that your guardian is shifting into gremlin mode due to fear. The equanimity scan in figure 15 can help you diagnose the root cause and return your guardian to its more constructive persona.

Muse's Agenda

The muse's agenda and core competencies are summarized in figure 14. The muse places its primary attention on matters of the heart. When its core energy is fueled by love, it shows up as the grand visionary and, of the three board members, is most identified with the construct of the inner child. The muse centered in love is in complete agreement with Frank Sinatra that "fairy tales can come true … when you're young at heart." When the muse forgets the truth of a reality based in love and oneness and chooses instead to become a victim to the lie of an illusion based in fear and a sense of separation, its core fear is the same two-part core fear of your other personal board members: I don't matter; I am powerless.

MEMBER: *Focus*	MUSE: *Heart*	
Love Persona	Visionary	
CORE FEAR	I DON'T MATTER I AM POWERLESS	
ATTRIBUTES	LOVE-BASED	FEARS
• Goal	Fun	Drudgery
• Means	Flexibility	Constraint
• Gift	Imagination	Monotony
• Passion	Play	Servitude
Fear Persona (GREMLIN)	Dilettante Sneak Wild Child Loose Cannon	
Defense Mechanism	Deceit and Rebellion	
Remedy	Find the Fun	

Figure 14: Muse's Agenda

The specifics of how that core fear manifests for the muse are aligned with the muse's love-based qualities and attributes. Its goal, or utmost desire, is having fun and believing life is a game. The specific fear that challenges that desire is drudgery: the possibility that anything—or worse yet, everything—is a grind. The muse is especially susceptible to stubbornness and avoidance when it perceives chores or toil.

The muse's means, or preferred way of fulfilling its desire for fun, is flexibility, believing maximizing freedom enhances everyone and everything. The specific fear that can test the muse's belief in the power of flexibility to maximize fun is constraint: any form of limitation, constriction, or restraint.

The muse's gift, greatest natural aptitude, and most valuable contribution to every situation is imagination. The specific fear that undercuts the muse's ability to demonstrate and contribute imagination is monotony of any sort: flatness, boredom, or tedium.

The muse's passion and chief delight—what brings the muse the most joy in life—is a sense of play: recreation and amusement. The specific fear that thwarts the muse's passion for play is any feeling of servitude: subservience, subjugation, or bondage.

When any or all of the muse's specific fears awaken the core fear that the muse does not matter or is powerless, it stops showing up as the grand visionary. Instead, it takes on one of its many gremlin personas, including the dabbling dilettante, sneak, wild child, or loose cannon.

The muse's initial passive aggressive technique to dissuade you from your chosen path is often a form of deceit. Avoidance and trickery are the tools of the frustrated muse. The dilettante and sneak personas are most common in this stage. When passive aggressive techniques prove ineffective, as the fear continues to grow, the muse will switch to more aggressive tactics of rebellion: the unsatisfied desire for *fun now* finding an outlet in a level of thrill-seeking abandon that introduces a risk of real and very un-fun harm. The fear is so unbearable that the muse will do anything to make it stop, including choosing activities and companions that are antithetical and horrifying to its sweet, fun-loving norm. The gremlin personas of the wild child and loose cannon are common in this stage.

There is a simple remedy for breaking this self-destructive cycle, leading the muse out of its fear-based, sabotaging gremlin persona and restoring it to love and a sense of oneness. The key is to help the muse *find the fun*. Not the adrenaline high of real danger. Just a small suggestion that with a little imagination, what appears to be drudgery could be transformed into something much easier than it appears. With a baby step in the right direction, the task might become downright entertaining. Fun is the medium in which the muse thrives. Fun will cause the muse's natural aptitudes and abilities to return, strengthen, and grow. When that happens, harmony and synergy with your other board members will be restored.

Whenever you start to feel whiny or put-upon, be alert for the possibility that your muse is shifting into gremlin mode due to fear. The equanimity scan in figure 15 can help you diagnose the root cause and return your muse to its more constructive persona.

Board Principles and Dynamics

If your board members could remain completely empowered by love in every moment, with deep and abiding respect for the full range of team strengths and perspectives, what a smooth and fulfilling life it could be. Your sage would channel an endless stream of brilliant insights, along with the wisdom to discern what should be pursued and when. Your muse would apply its creative genius to design the optimal way of communicating and manifesting those insights. Your guardian would serve as chief engineer to create, execute, monitor, and adjust the optimal plan for manifestation. No jealousy, no bickering, no sabotage. Just love-fueled collaboration with a single objective: to reveal and advance the highest good for all, in all, through all.

To achieve the more fluid and fulfilling life you seek, those are the board dynamics you are aiming for. Why does your board so often fall short of that goal, and what can you do to improve its functioning? Here are some additional insights to help you understand the elements of success, recognize when trouble is brewing, and employ the most reliable remedies to get things back on track quickly.

Gender Identity

In terms of gender, many clients sense the energetic gender of their board members long before they know their board members' names. Remember, we're not talking anatomy; we're talking male, female, and androgynous energy. One way to think of it is that male energy is more left brain, female is more right, and androgynous is a blend. There are many books on the subject of energetic gender. You can read them if you are so inclined, or you can trust your intuition. If it feels male, it probably is. If it feels female, it probably is. If it feels androgynous, it probably is. *Your* gender identity has nothing to do with the genders of your board members. They can all be male, all female, all androgynous, or mixed.

Choosing Names

That is a trick subtitle: you don't *choose* names for your board members. When they trust you and you are ready to connect with them more deeply, they will *tell you* their names. Honest. No, they aren't named after your first pet, your most memorable teacher, or members of your family—beloved or reviled. They have their own names, generally with very relevant etymologies. Once you know their names, if you look up the meanings and derivations, you'll find they hold great relevance to the roles they play and gifts they bring. Here are two quick examples in that regard.

The first example is my client Sarah who, as is so often the case, knew the names of her guardian and muse as soon as we began exploring the personal board/gremlin construct. She sensed a third distinct energy and described it as calm and wise but gave no name. Throughout our session, in an effort to help her tap into her intuition, I would say, "I'm sorry, I've forgotten the name of your sage. What is it?" She replied, "I told you. I don't know the name of my sage." I repeated variations on this tactic a couple more times during our forty-five-minute session and received the same reply. At the end of the session, as we were wrapping up, I said, "In looking over my notes, I realize I never wrote down the name of your sage." This time, she replied, "I have a name, but it doesn't make any sense." I encouraged her to ignore logic and trust her gut. She blurted out, "It's Sophia. But I don't even know anyone named Sophia." I became very still. "Sarah, do you or does anyone in your family have ties to Greece (language, travel, origin)?" She replied, "No." I told her, "Sophia means 'wisdom' in Greek. It's the name given to the wisdom aspect of God in the Bible. Congratulations, Sarah, I'm fairly certain your sage just told you her name."

The second example is my client Mark who also knew the names of his guardian and muse right off the bat. His sage's energy and name proved elusive over a period of weeks. Each week, we'd check in concerning his sage, and he'd report his sense that he'd made no progress. We would re-establish his intention to be open to connecting more deeply with his sage whenever it was ready to reveal itself. Then we would focus on other coaching matters. Periodically during sessions, I would try the techniques I used with Sarah and others ("I've forgotten your sage's name; I neglected to write down your sage's name; etc."). A number of weeks passed during which Mark had no awareness of the name. Then I received a midweek email from Mark, excitedly reporting that he had connected with his sage and knew her name. He said it was Sylvia. When he looked up the derivation of her name, he was blown away. Sylvia means "from the forest." Beginning at a very young age, when Mark was upset or frustrated by life, he would escape to the woods near his home for comfort. He has always loved being in the woods, whether camping, hiking, writing, or just thinking. Mark's sage had indeed introduced herself. She had been present in his life all along, leading him into the woods for solace.

Some clients know the names of their most dominant board member the moment we begin discussing the construct. Others know the guardian and muse right away because they have been listening to them bicker for decades. Some clients don't know any names for quite a while. One day, when your board member trusts you, it will tell you. It's like any other relationship that you hope will go to a more intimate level. As you prove to each board member that you are respectful, honorable, and committed to the long haul, they will each tell you their names in their own time.

It's not uncommon to have one member's name take longer than others. Often that member's set of competencies is the one you least value or most fear expressing. Don't expect any of them to tell you their names if your intention is to try to banish them the next time they pop their heads out of their foxholes by "going gremlin." Be patient, don't force it, and let your intuition tell you when it's time. Meanwhile, just do all of the things you already do to build other mutually respectful, trusting, and fulfilling relationships. Before you know it, you'll be engaging your board members in real-time, out-loud discussions and debates in the lobby of your favorite restaurant, boutique, or movie theater. They are eager to know you better too. They are just understandably skeptical about your motivations.

In the Beginning

When you and your board members were born, everything was love and light. The minute you began encountering opportunities for fear, the love and light began to unravel. Because you were small, young, and fairly helpless, those initial fears had a big impact, and your board members developed a tendency to overreact to perceived threats.

Life gets even riskier as you get older. As you grow and mature, life presents even more potential slings and arrows, and you present an ever-larger target for them to hit. If your board members become focused on all the fears, they can erroneously conclude that *everything* is dangerous and the only escape is to keep you as small and invisible as possible.

Why the Guardian Takes Over

There are two primary reasons why the guardian tends to take over early in life: First, survival is the top priority in the early years, and the guardian's specialty is safety and survival. Second, the guardian's proclivities for order, structure, and hard work make it popular with many cultures and parents. Raising a child is challenging. An obedient, predictable child makes the parents' job easier, though at a huge cost to the healthy development of that child into a confident, self-sufficient adult.

How the Muse Learns to Be Sneaky

For the very reasons that cultures and parents in general love the guardian's energy, many find the muse a handful. All that unbridled imagination, lack of fear, and willingness to experiment make raising a muse exhausting and downright scary at times. For that reason, many children get the message early on that to be popular and feel secure at home, they'd better learn to ratchet their muse back a few notches and toe the line. Those who do not can have a very tumultuous childhood. Even without any real threat of abuse or abandonment, many children learn early on to be seen and not heard.

To accomplish this long term, they must silence their muses. Because the guardian's prime directive is to keep you safe, often he will help the muse find a place to hide. I've facilitated deeply touching guardian/muse reconciliations with clients, including one where the guardian pulled a skeleton key out of his pocket so he could unlock the door to the closet where he and the muse agreed she would hide forty years earlier for the safety of the child.

Because all aspects of ourselves long to be expressed, even locked in a closet the typical muse will just find more devious ways to make its influence known. For its own energetic survival, the muse becomes quite adept at being sneaky.

Why the Sage Is Out to Lunch

Some clients think they don't have a sage. So far that hasn't proven to be the case. For the very reasons that guardians and muses tend to clash (egged on by our culture and parents), sages tend to hide. The constant discord is upsetting and discouraging to the sage's energetic constitution. When even its extraordinary gift of discernment proves ineffective at resolving conflict, the sage's first line of defense is withdrawal. If the discord continues to escalate such that it invades the sage's sanctuary, then it might change tactics and go ballistic, harming itself or others. Typically it just wants to be left alone, unless there is hope of reconciliation and a return to synergy. Be patient, trust your gut, and invite your sage to become active again in helping you discern the optimal path for your life and the best way to restore the guardian and muse to a relationship centered in love and light. A sage respectfully petitioned and offered an opportunity for hope will respond with greater courage in time.

Thorny Combinations

Sit with a copy of figure 11 and study the board members in pairs and as a team. Looking at their individual gifts, bear in mind that a virtue overdone becomes a defect. You will immediately see that the members are tailor-made to complement each other when fueled by love and drive each other nuts when fueled by fear. In the grip of fear, the guardian will become a control freak or drill sergeant, imposing a stranglehold of structure and discipline that will result in the muse (who loves flexibility) and the sage (who loves flow) going berserk. They'll then become afraid as well and retaliate in the only ways they know how, which will incite the guardian, and each other, to behave even more detrimentally.

Remember that any member "gone gremlin" will quickly pull your other board members out of alignment as well. Keep a watchful eye on each of them at all times and intervene the moment things feel at all off-kilter. The equanimity scan in figure 15 is an invaluable tool for managing the trickier permutations of their disparate agendas.

Keeping in mind the sensory balance teachings on relationships in the belonging section of chapter 5, you can also begin to imagine the added complexity that results from your board members' constant interaction with and reaction to the board members of everyone you encounter. Paying attention to what you're thinking, feeling, saying, and doing—and using the scan to identify and remedy any anomalies quickly and constructively—will go a long way to enjoying more loving, constructive, harmonious relationships with others. The relationship dynamics and opportunities of board members "gone Gremlin" is addressed in greater detail in my individual and group coaching programs. It will also receive considerable attention in my next book. Interpersonal gremlin dynamics are a powerful reminder that relationships are the doctoral program of life lessons.

A Personal Example

Now that you have a solid footing in personal board principles and dynamics, I will breathe additional life into the construct by sharing a story about one of the many ways they have shown up in my life recently.

The fifteen months before releasing this book were amazing for me. High productivity of the effortless centered-in-love kind, not the forced march variety. A nonstop shower of insights and opportunities, doors opening right and left, with me stepping across the portals in flow with confidence, enthusiasm, creativity, and serenity. These opportunities included

- hosting a monthly public access group coaching program sponsored by the Colorado Library System in Aurora;
- rebranding my practice under *Choose Your Energy: Change Your Life*;
- revamping and expanding my website;
- implementing a total of nine social media channels through which I publish regularly;
- writing my first book with Hay House/Balboa Press;
- producing a weekly talk radio show on VoiceAmerica's EmPOWERment Channel;
- doing multiple speaking engagements;
- completing ordination as a spiritual celebrant;
- being initiated as a Deeksha or oneness blessing giver;
- completing the Karuna level as a Reiki master teacher;
- being chosen by the city of Aurora as one of two local personalities with a three-page feature interview in the 2013 *Aurora Guide* (www.tiny.cc/djwauroraguide);
- building new individual and group coaching programs, seminars, and workbooks based on my Discovery Framework; and
- receiving a steady stream of new clients—individuals and groups.

I am honored by the calling the Universe has entrusted to me and grateful for Its never-ending flow of support. These developments have required lots of deep breathing and self-awareness. I've learned to demonstrate genuine respect for my personal board of directors—Claire, Ella, and Bee—when fear overtakes them and they shift into gremlin mode. Their clever and dire warnings have included such classics as, "Honey, it's been hard enough to keep you safe as it is. How are we going to manage to protect you if your presence in the Universe gets any bigger? You do this and you might as well paint a big old bull's-eye on your back for all the naysayers to aim at. You remember how badly that's gone in the past, right?"

When my clients report that their fears have reached up and grabbed them by the ankles yet again, I congratulate them. That means you are on the threshold of a big growth spurt, and your sage, guardian, and muse have "gone gremlin" because they are afraid they won't be able to keep you safe when you get that big. The answer?

- Seek to understand what old concerns have been brought out of hiding.
- Help them differentiate the remnants of past pain from today's reality.
- Remind them that *small* does not necessarily equal *safe* for an adult.
- Clarify that following your authentic path with love and without fear is what *safe* looks like now.
- Harness their loyalty.
- Leverage their core gifts of discernment, discipline, and imagination to keep moving yourself forward into a life you love.

So how did that particular scenario play out for me in January 2013? A while back, I recorded some unscripted radio interviews with a friend who is a professional radio personality. I loved the process and result so much that I set my intention to manifest a regular radio presence through which I could share my message of hope and possibilities more broadly and facilitate the ability of others to do likewise.

Just a few hours later, I received a call from a senior executive producer with VoiceAmerica, a leader in Internet broadcasting, inviting me to host a weekly sixty-minute talk radio program. During the final stages of completing my proposal, I reinforced my intention to express love, clarity, and energy. The result? Out of all the proposals submitted, I was one of three hosts invited to launch a new show on their new EmPOWERment channel in January.

I am often asked whether my board's gremlin energies are stirred up by big opportunities. Yes, when they choose to be gripped by fear, because that is what fear does to us. What do I do when that happens? I do what I encourage my clients to do. As with so many of the things I coach, the only way I know it works so well is that I have the opportunity to practice it myself with regularity:

- Pay attention and breathe.
- Engage with love, respect, curiosity, compassion, and gratitude.
- Reassure and redirect.
- Repeat as necessary.

The way to develop a stronger rapport with your board members and help them build more constructive working relationships with each other is to pay attention and get curious (two of the tools for fostering flow that we will cover in the next chapter). Meanwhile, here are some deeper insights into the nature of discernment, reason, and intuition.

Trusting Your Board's Discernment

Being able to trust your board members' discernment is the key to living a life of flow and equanimity. When your board is functioning optimally, you will be able to trust their discernment in all matters. Discernment consists of two components:

1. *Reason:* Assessment based on rational thinking.
2. *Intuition:* Insight beyond education, analysis, or logic, including but not limited to
   - clairvoyance (*seeing*),
   - clairsentience (*feeling/touching*),
   - clairaudience (*hearing/listening*),
   - clairalience (*smelling*),
   - claircognizance (*knowing*), and
   - clairgustance (*tasting*).

In our generally left-brain-exalting world, most of us have been taught to ignore intuition in favor of reason. At a minimum, we've been advised to validate intuition with reason before allowing ourselves to follow it. In her book *Sacred Contracts* (2003), Caroline Myss proposes that such a practice is the fast path to depression and madness. Intuition is a higher, deeper form of wisdom than reason. Authenticating intuition with reason is like using preschool constructs to validate a doctoral dissertation. In the words of Albert Einstein, "The intuitive mind is a sacred gift and the rational mind is a faithful servant. We have created a society that honors the servant and has forgotten the gift."

When your board members are fueled by love, you can trust their discernment—reasoning *and* intuition—to help you foster equanimity and access deepest wisdom to reveal and advance the highest good for all, by creating a moment-by-moment custom blend of competencies that varies based on the optimal mix for the opportunities in each life situation.

By way of another personal story, here is a real-life example of the power of trusting intuition over reason. Because I have substantial presentation experience, some of my professional advisors urged me early on to get my message of hope and possibilities on video for greater impact. Each time I considered doing so, energetically I felt either flat or overwhelmed by everything already on my plate. My rule concerning such things is not to assume resistance is a problem and never to use force.

When I feel myself resisting a new possibility, I stop and look with unflinching honesty at the energy underneath the situation. If I find fear or one of its cousins, I still don't use force to move myself forward. Instead, with a heaping dose of love, respect, curiosity, compassion, and gratitude for my thoughts and feelings, I refocus on understanding and transforming the fear into a more constructive fuel. Only after re-anchoring myself in a healthier place of love is it time to re-evaluate the opportunity itself.

If, on the other hand, I find no fear and only constructive energy underneath my resistance, then I respect my intuition and accept that there is a good reason not to move ahead with this particular idea at this particular time. In my wisest moments, I don't even invest energy trying to figure out what that reason might be. I simply trust my intuition because it represents a much greater wisdom than my lower order logical brain can produce, even on its most brilliant day.

Maybe I will have an experience or meet someone who will offer an important contribution to even greater success. Maybe moving further down other aspects of my current path first will result in this particular opportunity being moot or much easier later. Who knows? Who cares?

This was the case with me producing a video. When the idea was first suggested more than a year ago, it was a great idea; it just wasn't time yet. There were higher priority elements to build into the foundation of my practice before tackling videos, including robust proprietary content, additional technological comfort, and most important of all, substantial experience coaching a wide variety of people in a broad range of situations. Over a year later, when my energy finally supported me producing and releasing my first ever content in video and audio formats—a three-part series of five-minute *Tools for Fostering Flow* (available for free download at tiny.cc/djwfosterflow)—I achieved a much better result with far less effort and angst.

Developing these videos was a timely reminder of a key life lesson: always tune in to your energy and trust your intuition. Yet another opportunity to heed singer/songwriter Kathy Mattea's wise counsel, "Spread your wings, close your eyes, and always trust your cape!"

Equanimity Scan

Now that you have greater understanding of your board members' talents, perspectives, propensities, dynamics, and discernment, you are better equipped to notice when one or more of them becomes gripped by fear, and you know how best to return them to alignment with love.

Equanimity Scan

Pop the fear-based illusion of lies to restore the love-based reality of truth.
When gremlins arise, take a baby step toward restoring equanimity by determining
which member is feeling threatened based on which fears are being expressed.

√	Fear	Synonyms	What Love Looks Like	Likely Saboteur	How to Restore Love	Take Action
	Nihilism	Meaninglessness, Despair, Pessimism	Meaning			
	Discord	Arguing, Conflict, Friction	Synergy	Sage (Optimist)	See the Opportunity	
	Confusion	Bewilderment, Upheaval, Disorientation	Discernment			
	Force	Coercion, Pressure, Bullying	Flow			
	Danger	Jeopardy, Peril, Threat	Safety			
	Chaos	Anarchy, Pandemonium, Unruliness	Structure	Guardian (Engineer)	Make a Plan	
	Laziness	Lethargy, Sloth, Inertia	Discipline			
	Waste	Carelessness, Extravagance, Redundancy	Work			
	Drudgery	Chore, Grind, Toil	Fun			
	Constraint	Limitation, Constriction, Restraint	Flexibility	Muse (Visionary)	Find the Fun	
	Monotony	Flatness, Boredom, Tedium	Imagination			
	Servitude	Bondage, Subjugation, Subservience	Play			

Left vertical label: I DON'T MATTER—I AM POWERLESS
Center vertical label: I MATTER—I AM POWERFUL

© DJW Life Coach LLC 2012

Figure 15: Equanimity Scan

Figure 15 provides a simple form to guide this process. As with the other Discovery Framework scans, the process consists of five steps, with each step grounded in caring enough about yourself to do the following:

- Pay attention so that you notice quickly whenever fear creeps into your board's energetic mix.
- Invest your energy in assessing the root cause of the fear. Using the fears and synonyms listed on the left side of the form, identify which member or members may have become dysfunctional based on which fears align most closely with the way that member is wired. Realize that in any given difficult situation, one, two, or all three members may have fallen into the grips of their own particular fears. Understanding what's gotten each of them riled up is the best way to begin determining what can restore each of them to love and wholeness.

- Once you have identified the root fears at work, the love alternatives, and the board members involved, determine what baby steps will strengthen the presence of love in your board's energetic mix based on the scan's indicator of *how to restore love*. Especially in the case of the guardian, make sure any "plan" is a *baby step* and not an eighty-seven-point fifteen-year plan in fifteen-minute increments. Such a detailed plan might thrill the guardian, but it will introduce a new challenge as it sends the sage and muse screaming into the night. Likewise, overdoing it with the sage or muse is likely to throw one or both of the other two members into a tizzy. The optimal realignment approach will take into account the entire board as individuals and a team. The plan will be infused with understanding, balance, and harmony.
- Hold yourself accountable for following through on your commitment to take action.
- Assess your result and continuously refine and expand your action plan to maximize the presence of love and minimize the presence of fear in your board members' execution of their daily responsibilities.

When love takes over your core energy, you will begin building the less stressful, more fulfilling life you dream of. You are worth the effort.

As our initial exploration of your personal board of directors comes to a close, we shift our attention to a set of practical tools that will help you turn unconditional self-love and the Discovery Framework principles into healthy new habits that become a way of life.

For more insights into optimal synergy of intuition and reason, read *A Whole New Mind* by Daniel H. Pink.

Chapter 7:
Making It Happen—
Tools for Fostering Flow

If you are like many, at this point you are wondering, "The framework is elegant and intriguing but a bit complex. In practice, how do I work with my board of directors to apply the principles consistently enough to turn this way of living into a healthy new habit?" That is precisely where my tools for fostering flow come into play (figure 16).

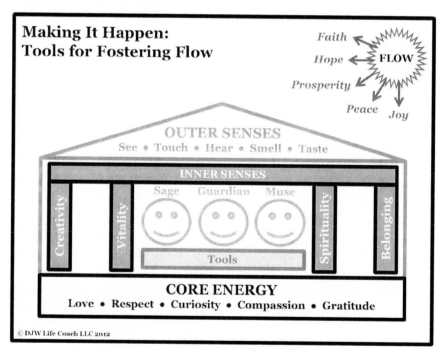

Figure 16: Tools for Fostering Flow

This set of simple personalized practices helps you realize the essential shift from *believing* these principles in your *head* to *living* them from your *heart*. Making these tools a way of life helps you stay centered in flow. And when you drift off center occasionally, as any of us can do when overwhelmed by stress and gripped by ancient self-destructive scripts, these tools are the key to recognizing it quickly and getting back on track easily.

You have already encountered many tools in the previous chapters. Here, for easy access, are fourteen of my favorites:

1. **Pay Attention:** If you don't recognize you're feeling stressed, you can't change it. Practice mindfulness by noticing what you are thinking, feeling, saying, and doing and figuring out why.

2. **Breathe:** Next time things start getting a little crazy, stop, take three deep breaths, become fully present, restore sanity, and realize you have options. Your brain needs oxygen to function effectively. Try setting a timer on your phone or computer to remind you periodically to stop, close your eyes for a minute, and just breathe.

3. **Be Here Now:** Forget rehashing the past and agonizing over the future. This moment is your only real opportunity to make a difference. Just you, just here, just now, just be. Perpetual equanimity and fulfillment come from dancing in the moment.

4. **Opportunity Knocks:** While life won't always follow your plans and expectations, everything in life *is* an opportunity. An opportunity to understand yourself better, open your heart wider, and develop greater compassion for yourself and others. While the details of our lives differ, we all experience the same range of emotions, from fear, frustration, and loneliness to joy, contentment, and peace. With yourself firmly planted in the present moment, it is your ability to respond creatively and constructively that makes the difference.

5. **Get Curious:** If everything is an opportunity, where might the opportunity be in this situation? The Universe is far more creative than we can imagine. Assume the best and look for the silver lining in even the darkest cloud.

6. **Talk to Yourself:** It is the smartest crazy thing you'll ever do.

It improves your sense of perspective, creativity, and humor. You might discover that what you were dreading isn't likely to happen or will be much easier than you feared. With a little imagination, it might even be a great opportunity. This tool is particularly effective for constructively engaging, understanding, and motivating your sage, guardian, and muse.

7. **Write It Down:** Getting stressful thoughts out of your head and onto paper can also improve your sense of perspective. Often, just putting them in writing reduces them to a more manageable size.

8. **Move It:** When in doubt, move about. A gentle walk around the room, the block, or the gym will begin releasing natural tranquilizers and restoring full breathing. It feeds your creativity so you will be able to come up with more resourceful options for handling your situation.

9. **Hydrate:** Water fosters flow and sustains life. It composes up to 60 percent of the average human body and covers 70 percent of the earth's surface. Drink. Shower. Bathe. Swim. Cry. Hydrate yourself in every way imaginable and watch yourself flow through the ups and downs of life with greater flexibility, creativity, and resilience.

10. **Trust Your Gut:** You have inside you all the wisdom you seek. Instead of stressing yourself out by fighting your instincts or feeling compelled to justify your hunches with logic, try trusting your intuition instead.

11. **Behave As If:** There are two aspects to this one: If you gave yourself the same care and attention you give your friends and loved ones, what support would you give yourself right now? And what would you dare to do if you believed you couldn't fail?

12. **Take Baby Steps:** Slow and steady produces meaningful, lasting results. Vast forced output is rarely sustained. Great strides of lasting value involve myriad baby steps over time. If the conceivers of the Taj Mahal had believed fast was the only way to get there, it would have crumbled in the first storm. Your dreams are the same. Don't try to take them all on at once. Identify the next small step and take it. Then another and another and another. Before you know it, you will have built your dream, and it will last your whole life through.

13. **Celebrate:** Every step forward is a cause for celebration. Every time you move closer to your dreams, pat yourself on the back with a party moment. Ta-da! A steady stream of self-affirmation will continue releasing additional positive fuel to keep you moving forward.

14. **Time for What Matters:** Time is not a scarce resource. You have all the time you need for the things that matter. Your sole responsibility in each moment is to discern what matters most right now, to focus, and to follow through. Using the other tools will help clear the way to accessing your deepest wisdom and moving forward, in each moment, with confidence, peace, and joy.

Having completed the overview of the Discovery Framework, this is a great time to stop, close your eyes, and take a few deep breaths. Remember, our approach is to take it easy. Continue to let the constructs gently wash over and through you without any need to force their implementation.

The framework provides a path to a life of freedom based in flow rather than a life lived at the effect of any fears that may have taken root within yourself or in those around you. No longer tossed by the winds and waves of circumstance, you will learn to live anchored in the power and surety of love in every moment. Love is never about force. It is always about flow.

The next section of the book includes nine Lessons in Living based on the experiences of my clients. The lessons provide examples of how real people just like you transformed the framework from a set of principles that made sense intellectually to precepts they live by every day.

Relax into their messages of hope and transcendence, knowing in your heart that you too can create the more fulfilling life you dream of. By fueling your core energy with love, respect, curiosity, compassion, and gratitude, you too can foster a life of generous, effortless, gracious flow filled with faith, hope, prosperity, peace, and joy.

For more insights into recognizing and cultivating opportunities, read *The Art of Possibility* by Rosamund Stone Zander and Benjamin Zander.

Part III:
Lessons in Living

Failure to take care of your own health will inevitably mean you will be unable to care for the ones you love. Though the damage can be very slow in showing up, one day you wake up weighed down by a load you can no longer bear—physically, mentally, emotionally, or spiritually.

When the connection between how we show up in the world and who we are at our core becomes weaker and weaker, our personal orbit becomes askew, and only a significant repositioning can put us back in touch and back on track.

What if your dogged persistence in your current, incredibly painful situation is not fueled by courage but by fear? What if you are the only one keeping you from exploring and enjoying the life you long for?

When we help them pop the bubble of illusion filled with fear-based lies and embrace a reality filled with the truth of love-based flow, our personal board members shake off their gremlin personas and return to their constructive roles in our lives.

None of us can know what is possible until we are willing to let go of what no longer serves our highest good and relax into the seeming void of transition. In just such a way, we create the possibility for shedding our personal chrysalises, thereby allowing our lives to take flight.

Life is an endless cycle of transition, honoring what has been, cherishing what is, and learning when and how to say good-bye while keeping our hearts open to an unknown future that has yet to reveal itself. We are all always in some stage of transition.

Setting an intention is not about a short- or long-term goal— something you will be "doing" in the future. Instead, when you set your intention, you focus on how you are "being" in the present moment.

Every time you walk away from the creative activities that feed your spirit by telling yourself, "Fun doesn't matter," you take another step closer to the life you dread: a life of restricted activity and lower energy with a resigned, melancholy spirit. Every time you tell yourself your best days are behind you, you create a self-fulfilling prophecy.

A powerful way to turn on the light of love within you and keep it burning brightly is to ask yourself many times each day, "If I were my own beloved child or valued client, how would I take care of me right now?"

Never treat what is true for someone else as your personal truth; instead listen with respect, curiosity, and discernment. Connecting deeply with others allows for the possibility that they will awaken within you a personal truth that lies sleeping.

Chapter 8:
Foundation

The insights offered in the lessons in this chapter, in combination with those provided in part 1, will help you build a firm foundation for your Journey to Wholeness—the grand adventure of falling in love with yourself more deeply every day.

The Lesson of the Blocks

Have you ever watched a baby or a toddler play with a stack of blocks? For a child, the experience is sheer delight. They are free to pile them up, change them, rearrange them, or dump them in a heap if that is their pleasure. *Adult blocks are a very different matter.*

Most of the barriers to pursuing and achieving our desires in life are not caused by immovable, external blocks but by inner blocks formed from limiting beliefs we have manufactured for ourselves or assimilated from others. Many of our limiting beliefs were acquired from constraints imposed by our country, culture, religion, family, or the media. We created other limitations as a result of our own lack of imagination, shortage of curiosity, or insufficiently healed past traumas. Gremlins are an especially strong form of limiting beliefs exhibited by members of our personal boards of directors.

Though the specific origins vary, all of these limiting beliefs share a common energetic source: fear. When we choose to fuel ourselves with more constructive core energy grounded in love, respect, curiosity, compassion, and gratitude, we can eliminate our fear-based limiting beliefs and transform our lives into the more fulfilling ones we long for.

I first met my client Diana during my career as an organization transformation consultant. When she reconnected with me again more than twenty years later, she was struggling under the weight of a diverse and robust collection of inner blocks. She didn't call them that. She just knew she was unhappy and couldn't see a way out.

One of the most serious assumptions in Diana's collection was the firm belief that you only get one chance at success. Even though she had been successful in many different jobs and had run a small business for years, she believed that she was *always* just one mistake away from setting off a chain reaction of relentless failures of cataclysmic proportions—at least in her own mind. Her failure wouldn't be an event; she would *be* a failure.

People who bear the burden of this assumption go through life looking for some insurance—someone or something to protect them from making the "ultimate" mistake. They may decide that the answer is taking more courses, securing another professional credential, or partnering with someone else who appears more self-assured (but may turn out to be more confident than competent). Grasping at straws, the Dianas of the world reach outside themselves—to another person, thing, or experience—to find a sense of security and peace.

"I thought that I'd finally found my silver bullet," Diana said. "After years of running my small business, the economy tanked, and I was having trouble keeping it all going. Until a friend and colleague suggested that perhaps we should set up a new business and operate as partners. I was thrilled! I held this woman in high regard and thought she would be the perfect protection against my destiny of making the one unrecoverable mistake.

"By the time I started coaching with Deborah, my wonderful partner/safety net had turned into an albatross. Unable to make a decision or move forward, my partner took analysis paralysis to a whole new level. I could only conclude that I must have made a grotesque mistake in my calculations somewhere.

"When I talked to Deborah about the situation, it had already been going on for months. Absolutely nothing was getting done. My fear was many times larger than it had been when at a minimum I could count on myself and did not have to wait for someone else to test every possible option before making even the smallest decision."

At the heart of Diana's fear lay her bag lady gremlin with its "one mistake" assumption. She had little chance of escaping when that conversation began playing in her head.

Instead of enjoying her life, she was working like a lunatic, trying to stave off disaster. She was wearing herself out with no understanding of what was driving her. "I couldn't get out of my own way," Diana said, telling me that in spite of all the evidence to the contrary, working with this partner was her one chance for success. She just had to keep trying to make it work, however improbable that now seemed.

Eventually I asked the question that has become Diana's mantra: "How can you know that? How can you be sure that this partnership is your one and only chance for success?"

In the silence that followed, I asked again ever so gently, "What if you're mistaken? What if you have lots of other possibilities for success, maybe even better ones? What if your dogged persistence in your current incredibly painful situation is not fueled by courage but by fear? What if you're the only one keeping you from exploring and enjoying the life you long for?"

In that moment, Diana remembered what Austrian neurologist, psychiatrist, and Holocaust survivor Viktor Frankl said: "Between stimulus and response there is a space. In that space is our power to choose our response. In our response lies our growth and our freedom."

The work Diana has done and continues to do has opened that space for her in so many situations. Space in which she asks herself questions and shows herself compassion. Space in which she can challenge a gremlin, recognize a limiting belief, or simply take a deep breath.

"It's an amazing thing how much change you can achieve when you shift your energy and begin the work of building the life you want to live," Diana said. "While I'm still working on it, I no longer worry about money, failure, and bag-lady-hood before I even open my eyes in the morning! I am excited about where I can go from here and know that Deborah can continue to help me find the peace and joy that can make my life sing.

"Though I still have plenty of work to do, I have learned to say, 'You can't know that,' whenever a limiting belief or gremlin rears its head. I know that my willingness to 'do the work' is essential to success. But I also know that when you are on a difficult journey, it is wise to have a guide who knows the way."

Equipped with greater self-awareness, a broader sense of possibilities, and a stronger belief in herself, Diana dissolved her business partnership and headed off in a new direction with her own firm. She even decided to move to a place where she would have the ability to spend more time with family and take her life in new directions. All of this was fueled by the inspiration, vitality, and determination she unleashed when she stopped wasting her energy in fear, worry, and doubt.

Diana is living proof of Eddie Robinson's assertion, "The will to win, the desire to succeed, the urge to reach your full potential ... these are the keys that will unlock the door to personal excellence."

For more insights into the power of belief, read *The Power of Positive Thinking* by Norman Vincent Peale.

The Lesson of the Gremlin

What do you think of when you hear the word *gremlin*? For many, it conjures up an image from childhood nightmares, and one of its definitions is actually "bogeyman": the monster lurking under the bed. It didn't start out that way. The origin of the word *gremlin* is usually credited to pilots in World War II who jokingly blamed mechanical failures on small imaginary monsters they dubbed gremlins. Over time, however, books and movies created some frightening and not-so-harmless gremlins. However, long before the word *gremlin* existed, we all had them. We just didn't know it.

In chapter 6 we talked at some length about the tendency of your personal board members to exhibit their gremlin personas when gripped by fear. The term *gremlin* is used as a metaphor for a part of us that is neither inherently evil nor intentionally harmful but a deeply rooted pattern of behavior triggered by our oldest most painful scenarios and a deep need to protect ourselves by any means necessary.

Our board members take their jobs very seriously. When they first give birth to their gremlin personas, their mission is simple: to protect us from ever again experiencing painful or embarrassing situations. As we get older and our lives become more complex, our board members see that many situations, while different in details, offer the same opportunity for pain. As their fears continue to grow, so do the possibilities for gremlin interference by board members who expand their job definition to include any situation or person who could ever lead to discomfort. Talk about limiting our world. The great irony is that when in the grip of fear, gremlins will do whatever it takes—including some very underhanded tactics—in order to protect us from the potential danger "out there." In this way, they become the enemy within.

Some "protect" us by sabotaging every potentially intimate relationship, thus escaping the risk—and joy—that intimacy brings. Some protect us by remembering every disappointing new experience in our past, painting every future opportunity with the same brush.

A new job might remind your sage, guardian, or muse of situations in the past where an authority figure was frightening, dangerous, or just plain unkind. As a result, its gremlin persona will be on the prowl at every new job, looking for the boss it remembers so well from the past. By leading with the same expectations, we are nearly guaranteed to attract the energy we transmit.

As we discovered in chapter 6, gremlins are the voices of our most deeply embedded fears, with personalities and names all their own. Like the weeds in your garden, effective long-term management of gremlins is not about elimination of surface behaviors. Lopping your gremlins off at the surface with the weed whacker of denial or superficial behavior change may yield a more cosmetic result temporarily. But because they are tenacious and deep-rooted, they usually grow back quickly. And with each failed attempt at superficial removal, they are likely to expand their purview of peril even further.

There are more effective and lasting measures we can take to neutralize and redirect our gremlins' relentless, misguided, ever-escalating interference. When we help them pop the bubble of illusion filled with fear-based lies and embrace a reality filled with the truth of love-based flow, our personal board members shake off their gremlin personas and return to their constructive roles in our lives.

My client Anne worked in a particular job for nine years but was very unhappy. Despite her best efforts, she kept hitting roadblocks. She knew she was spinning her wheels and was becoming increasingly frustrated.

What to do? Stick it out and keep trying? Find another job in the same industry? Or a similar job in a different industry? Or retrain for a totally different kind of job? She'd tried these and other avenues in the past, and though the surface details differed, she seemed to keep ending up in essentially the same situation.

"I've never been a quitter. I have always been a person who slogged through whatever muck life threw in my path, and tried to make it better," said Anne. "I'd begun to wonder if I was just born unlucky, landing in one toxic environment after another, or was it possible that I was getting in my own way?"

In the midst of this self-examination, Anne's friend Kathleen approached her with an exciting opportunity. Kathleen had decided to semiretire and said, "I want you to apply for my job."

Kathleen was well respected by her employees and by the organization she served as managing partner. Finding herself at a time in her own career when she felt neither valued nor successful, Anne was surprised and flattered that her friend believed she had the leadership qualities the new job required. Kathleen was committed to leaving a much-loved job in trusted hands—*Anne's hands.*

While engaged in internal debate over this job opportunity, Anne learned about my practice of conducting complimentary coaching sessions with prospective clients. She saw that this might be yet another opportunity: the chance to engage a trusted professional partner in confronting head-on whether her frustrations were just bad luck or a pattern of self-sabotage.

"When I started working with Deborah, I felt drained by all the aggravation that had built up over the years. While there was exhilaration in starting a new job because Kathleen was my friend and had shown such high regard for me, it felt especially important this time to be clear about what I was doing and why.

"Deborah and I began with a sixty-minute complimentary session during which she coached me on real issues of my choosing. The session was so powerful that I invested in a weekly coaching relationship and the Energy Leadership Index assessment to give myself a fighting chance at changing my past pattern. Coaching with

Deborah using the Energy Leadership paradigm gave me hope—a new language and a new model for making sense of my life."

As she began her journey with me, Anne looked back on the journals she'd kept over the years and got depressed by reading them: they sounded like a broken record. I call this a *gremlin alert*; finding evidence of consistent self-sabotage is a valuable step in recognizing the part a gremlin may be playing in your life. Anne was intrigued by the possibility of making friends with her guardian and its gremlin persona, Sister Mary Perfect, so named for its need to get everything just right—at work, at home, in relationships, or in any other aspect of living.

As our coaching sessions progressed from week to week, I brought a great deal of curiosity into the sessions, encouraging Anne's ability to be playful, inquisitive, vulnerable, and respectful toward herself, everyone, and every situation. Anne also began to get clarity about the way in which things she had experienced in the past might be playing out repeatedly in the present.

One of the most powerful exercises, according to Anne, was stepping back and looking at the job she had just left to try to find commonalities between that job situation and others, or that job situation and childhood experience. Was there a theme that appeared in each of her life stories?

Parallels began to emerge as she thought about family relationships, the role she'd played, and how she had continued to re-enact that role as an adult. Perhaps some of her boss's behaviors reminded her of a parent's behavior, creating uncertainty, embarrassment, and internal friction. After our conversations, Anne said she would hang up the phone and simply stare into space, blown away by the power of what she was discovering and feeling.

"Deborah's intuition and comprehensive notes were invaluable for maintaining continuity from one session to another. Without them, it would have been a much more difficult and lengthy undertaking to put the pieces together and begin to recognize patterns. Week by week, I began seeing myself differently. I came to understand that because life is not a destination but a journey that unfolds, I didn't need to have all the answers in every moment."

One of the great gifts Anne has experienced in her new job is the magic that can happen when she stops trying to do everything perfectly herself and instead becomes a consultative, open, and curious manager, offering employees the opportunity to be real contributors to a successful team.

"Something they'd known with Kathleen and that I have actually succeeded in recreating. My experience of life was transformed once I learned to embrace every moment, curious about all the possibilities rather than scanning for all the tigers in the bushes.

"A friend recently said to me, 'This is what you've been training for—been waiting for—all your life.' And it's true. With Deborah's help, I've embraced my guardian and have been able to see both the good things she brings into my life as well as the challenges she creates whenever, in gremlin mode, she assumes each day or experience is inherently dangerous."

It is essential to remember that effective gremlin work can never be forced. It surfaces organically when you are ready. Nowhere is the application of love, respect, curiosity, compassion, and gratitude more vital than when engaging the members of your personal board of directors. Remember that their gremlin activity is actually good news. It means you are on the verge of a big breakthrough in personal growth. Your sage, guardian, or muse "go gremlin" because they are afraid they won't be able to keep you safe when you get that big. Remember the steps to soothing their fears:

- Seek to understand what old concerns have been brought out of hiding.
- Help them differentiate the remnants of past pain from today's reality.
- Remind them that *small* does not necessarily equal *safe* for an adult.
- Clarify that following your authentic path with love and without fear is what *safe* looks like now.
- Harness their loyalty.
- Leverage their core gifts of discernment, discipline, and imagination to keep moving yourself forward into a life you love.

Anne agrees wholeheartedly: "It's not as though I had a split personality. Before my gremlin work, like many people, I just had a set of counterproductive behaviors that could be easily triggered by any sense of risk to me. Now I have the self-awareness and objectivity to stop before reacting instinctively and determine whether a new situation is indeed like an old one, or perhaps it's yet another opportunity to expand my horizons and try something new."

For more insights into releasing yourself from the limitations of ancient scripts, read *Excuses Begone!* by Dr. Wayne W. Dyer.

The Lesson of the Butterfly

Throughout the world—and throughout time—the butterfly has been a symbol of dramatic transformation. It is easy to see why: no longer earthbound, a new creature emerges from its chrysalis utterly and completely changed, spreading its glorious wings as if knowing all along it was born to fly. In the words of Maya Angelou, "We delight in the beauty of the butterfly but rarely admit the changes it has gone through to achieve that beauty." Those changes don't begin in the chrysalis. That is just one of many steps on the journey to becoming a butterfly.

Once fully grown, the caterpillar seems to know instinctively when it is time to move on. Unlike humans, whose forward movement is often blocked with assumptions and self-doubt, the caterpillar simply does what it was born to do: It positions itself for the next step in its journey. It creates a button of silk to fasten its body to a leaf or twig. Once it attaches itself, the old skin comes off, revealing a hard skin called a chrysalis. Once it is safely within the chrysalis and positioned for change, an extraordinary process begins. Just as the caterpillar knew when it was time to move on to the chrysalis stage, the fledgling butterfly will know when it is time to leave the chrysalis and take flight.

It is the same with human beings. The potential for transformation is always there, however hampered we may feel by limiting beliefs and raw fear. In the words of Richard Buckminster Fuller, "There is nothing in a caterpillar that tells you it's going to be a butterfly." None of us can know what is possible until we are willing to let go of what no longer serves our highest good and relax into the seeming void of transition. In just such a way, we create the possibility for shedding our personal chrysalises, thereby allowing our lives to take flight. As Richard Bach reminds us, when we trust in the *unfolding* of our highest good at all times, we find, "What the caterpillar calls the end of the world, the Master calls the butterfly."

My client Sarah feels the most important changes she has made in her life are becoming more self-aware and learning how to use that new awareness in all aspects of her life.

"I started working with Deborah when I was training to become a life coach myself. I had absolute faith in the coaching process and knew that all world-class coaches have coaches of their own. My initial goals for our coaching relationship were focused on optimizing my performance as a coach—what I needed to understand about myself and how I could leverage my personal insights and experience to partner with my clients on their journeys. I wasn't looking for personal change, just greater professional understanding and perspective. Oh my! Be careful what doors you open; the Universe will deliver.

"One of the coaching insights I gained in our initial sessions was how to leverage my life experience to benefit the client without sharing my personal stories directly. As I saw Deborah keep the focus on my story, not hers, by using her experience to inspire the wise questions she asked me, I knew I could do the same with my clients."

As my work with Sarah went deeper, it became obvious that she may not have known herself as well as she thought. In fact, if anyone had said she was a person who had built and maintained a nearly impregnable barrier around herself, she would have said they were mistaken. Yet as we examined her self-awareness, energy, and spirituality together, we identified a pattern of situations where the help and support of others would have made her journey less stressful and more joyful. Like so many of us, Sarah had developed a habit of shutting others out, thinking she was "protecting them." Over time, she came to recognize that she was really trying to *protect herself* by keeping her guard up and staying "small" because doing otherwise just felt "too big" and vulnerable for her.

"Deborah penetrated that guard by asking gentle, respectful questions, demonstrating the love, respect, curiosity, compassion, and gratitude that are the bedrock of her coaching approach. Amazing what some compassionate, probing questions can reveal!" Sarah said.

"A prime example was my divorce. Making the decision to pursue a divorce required a three- to four-year journey of deep and agonizing soul-searching. During that gut-wrenching process, I told no one and dealt with the pain myself, thinking I was protecting the people I cared about.

"As Deborah and I uncovered more and more situations and events that might trigger putting my guard up in the future, that weird, uncomfortable feeling in my belly told me we were on to something very big. Life was delivering a major opportunity to stop, contemplate, and act upon what I was learning."

With reflection, Sarah began to realize that what she had created was not a supportive chrysalis of transformation but a barricade of isolation. Butterflies do not experience the chrysalis as a barrier but as a pathway for growing into who they always were deep inside. They know instinctively it is a nurturing place of profound, transformative growth from which they emerge in a completely natural way when the time is right.

"Becoming self-aware brought mixed emotions and took me out of my comfort zone," Sarah said. "But replacing the metaphor of a 'barricade' with that of a chrysalis helped me see that the potential for transformation was right there all along and well worth the effort."

For more insights into the transformative power of the chrysalis in human experience, read *When the Heart Waits* by Sue Monk Kidd.

Chapter 9:
Core

Having built a firm foundation based on the insights in the previous lessons, those offered in this chapter will help you strengthen your energetic core to better support your Journey to Wholeness. As with exercise for your physical core, these lessons will help you feel more centered by improving your energetic alignment, balance, stability, and strength.

The Lesson of Core Strength

According to fitness experts, many people are not familiar with the term "core strength training" or they think it refers only to six-pack abs. Sports Fitness Advisor's description is much broader:

> Core strength training may be a relatively new, buzz term in the fitness industry but coaches and athletes have understood its value for many years. The core region consists of far more than just the abdominal muscles. In fact core strength training aims to target all the muscle groups that stabilize the spine and pelvis. It's these muscle groups that are critical for the transfer of energy from large to small body parts during many sporting activities (2013).

My client Lori could easily be a poster child for core training. She works out at the gym regularly, not to mention completing sixty-mile bike rides on the weekends and a run along the water several times a week. Even so, in Lori's book, real core strength training takes more than cardio, ab, and back work. In her words, "The real core is even further in."

While many might be envious of Lori's healthy weight and physical fitness, she's a perfect example that being lean and fit is not a guarantee for feeling fulfilled and whole.

If you encountered Lori in person, you would see a smart, successful, attractive woman who appears to have it all together. You might even feel a twinge of resentment that she makes it look so easy, but her genuine thoughtfulness, authenticity, and gentle heart are irresistible. Those who know her well marvel that she retains that authentic kindness in the face of the challenges she has experienced over the years.

At one point, Lori was on the verge of bankruptcy, having gone from an extraordinary net worth to serious trouble. It certainly wasn't from excessive spending or waste. Lori was always a saver and independently built her net worth through hard work and successful investments. Prior to the US economic meltdown, her years of careful saving and frugal living were paying off. Then, overnight, the real estate crisis transformed many of her investments from assets to liabilities.

During that difficult time, a man who had been her friend for ten years became more, and they moved in together. It's amazing what you discover when you live with someone. Over time, it became obvious to her that even a long-term friendship did not necessarily segue into a healthy intimate relationship. Even so, she didn't give up easily. Her nature is to assess any problem and try to fix it, even if the problem lies well outside her control.

The one-two punch of devastating financial results and a deeply disappointing relationship took a toll on core strengths that had long enabled Lori to quickly solve problems and put things right. The most devastating casualty was a loss of trust in herself. That distrust began spreading like a virus until she was questioning not just her financial and relationship judgment but nearly every decision she faced.

Eventually, the level of her personal discomfort told her things had to change. But she couldn't seem to find her way back to trusting herself and knowing she was "enough." At the recommendation of a friend, Lori visited my website and read the success stories of others who had worked with me.

"I finally recognized that I needed a 'tune-up,'" Lori said. "I had paid attention to personal growth for many years, immersing myself in the work of Dr. Wayne W. Dyer, Deepak Chopra, and others. Nonetheless, somehow I had somehow gotten off track.

"My first conversation with Deborah 'sold me.' Step-by-step, our work together provided me with much-needed course corrections to deal with the distrust and discomfort I was feeling. I learned that recognizing those feelings and dealing with them was an important first step toward the changes I desired. Carving the time for coaching out of my endless to-do list was an important commitment to and investment in my relationship with myself."

Somewhere along the way, Lori stopped trusting herself and started measuring herself by other people's opinions and standards. We talked at length about the five agreements of spiritual teacher and author don Miguel Ruiz based on ancient Toltec wisdom. In his book *The Fifth Agreement* (2010), he suggests using doubt as a tool to discern the truth. He wisely counsels never to treat what is true for someone else as your personal truth; instead, listen with respect, curiosity, and discernment. There is no need to be afraid of listening to others, since you always have the ability to apply your own discernment and determine if what you hear resonates with *your* truth. Connecting deeply with others allows for the possibility that they will awaken within you a *personal truth* that lies sleeping.

Suddenly the fact that Lori had doubts about herself was not necessarily a problem but a gift. Lori found the strength to terminate the relationship that was sapping her energy and eroding her confidence. She took thoughtful, careful, gentle steps that led to a compassionate and clean break. Her relief at "getting herself back" was powerful and palpable.

"The most important change I've made is turning my focus inward for answers and strength. I needed to be reminded not to look to others to convince me of my own value."

When Lori said "the real core is even further in," she was referring to the fact that long before a "strong core" described physical fitness, the term was used to describe a different kind of strength. The strength it takes to trust yourself, to find wisdom within, and to live by the light of your own truth.

> *As soon as you trust yourself, you will know how to live.*
> —*Johann Wolfgang von Goethe*

> *When I'm trusting and being myself ... everything in my life reflects this by falling into place easily, often miraculously.*
> —*Shakti Gawain*

> *If you really put a small value upon yourself, rest assured that the world will not raise your price.*
> —*Author unknown*

> *A person who doubts himself is like a man who would enlist in the ranks of his enemies and bear arms against himself. He makes his failure certain by himself being the first person to be convinced of it.*
> —*Alexandre Dumas*

> *You are Braver than you Believe, Smarter than you Seem, and Stronger than you Think.*
> —*Winnie the Pooh*

As Lori continues to live her truth, her self-confidence, self-esteem, and finances continue to improve. She is making clear choices about everything from her career to a long-troubled relationship with her parents. She has begun fostering a guide dog for a local charity—a long-buried desire that has the potential to bring self-fulfillment, laughter, and energy into her life. Until she honored and made room for it, that dream had remained a quiet wish that sat in her heart, waiting for its time to come.

For more insights into the power of ancient Toltec wisdom, read *The Four Agreements* and *The Fifth Agreement* by don Miguel Ruiz.

The Lesson of Baby Steps

When we use the term *baby steps*, we often do so with an inherent judgment, as though someone taking *baby steps* forward is not to be taken seriously. Imagine a news story that describes one politician's plan as making "great strides" while another's represents only "baby steps." Our inner judge might well interpret that to mean that the second politician is perhaps too cautious and uncertain while the first is confident and self-assured and knows where he is going.

The truth of the matter, however, is that we underestimate what it takes to make baby steps. Babies and toddlers, the baby step experts, experience the world at a heightened level of awareness, using all of their senses to take in new data and expand their knowledge base to achieve new goals. Maybe we denigrate baby steps because their goal is often a simple one: a parent's hug, a much-loved toy, a cookie, or just a frolic in the direction of greater freedom.

The fact is that the wild, wobbly gait of the new walker defies our assessment that baby steps are cautious. They are not. They are bold and intrepid, risking injury or failure with hope and a brave heart.

When adults take baby steps to improve their lives, they are always on journeys of great courage and importance. In fact, some very famous people have honored the small destination-conscious steps that move all of us forward.

> *What saves a man is to take a step. Then another step.*
> —Antoine de Saint-Exupery

> *Take the first step in faith. You don't have to see the whole staircase, just take the first step.*
> —Martin Luther King, Jr.

> *Success seems to be connected with action. Successful people keep moving. They make mistakes, but they don't quit.*
> —Conrad Hilton

> *Whoever wants to reach a distant goal must take small steps.*
> —Helmut Schmidt

I dream of men who take the next step instead of worrying about the next thousand steps.
— *Theodore Roosevelt*

Your mind, this globe of awareness, is a starry universe. When you push off with your foot, a thousand new roads become clear.
— *Rumi, thirteenth-century Persian poet*

My client Lily will proudly tell you that she "walked [her] way out of depression, taking baby steps, one at a time." Lily is someone who would be described as strong but not aggressive. Giant strides are not her style. She is contemplative and serious—an introvert with a wry wit and a surprising humility about a lifetime of accomplishments.

Lily and I first worked together when she participated in a life transitions group I facilitated. When the group sessions were complete, she chose to continue her personal growth work with me one-on-one.

"That discussion group set my feet on a spiritual journey. Along the way I discovered, as many people do, that my spiritual journey had actually started long before. I just didn't recognize it until I stood in the backwash of many traumatic years and felt ready at last to see the path I was on," Lily said.

"The focus of the discussion group was 'The Art of Change: Flourishing in Uncertain Times.' The insights resonated with me so powerfully that I knew I needed to continue exploring where I was and what the next steps might be. I'd gained some new language and tools and could see an *open* door before me where I'd never even noticed a door before."

Life is actually an endless cycle of transition—honoring what has been, cherishing what is, learning when and how to say good-bye while keeping our hearts open to an unknown future that has yet to reveal itself. Promotion or layoff. Marriage or divorce. A new birth or an empty nest. Experiencing serious health challenges or a success we're not sure we'll be able to handle. We are all always in some stage of transition. Lily did an excellent job of describing one of the challenges for people in transition: they not only don't see an *open* door, but they often can't see any door *at all*.

The transition from that discussion group to working with a life coach was a baby step that would turn out to be extremely powerful. While Lily had known me personally for more than a year, she wasn't familiar with life coaching at all. Like many others, she found that this insight-filled modality helped her recognize blocks and strengthen her own self-awareness. In her words, "Without self-awareness, you not only don't see the blocks, but you also don't see the opportunities."

Although at the outset she couldn't articulate *precisely* what she hoped to accomplish by working with me, Lily trusted and followed her own intuition, certain she had gotten a glimpse of that open door and wanted to know how to step through it.

Over time, she used her growing self-awareness to identify dreams and goals that were no longer black and white but filled with color and a new energy.

"I knew that energy didn't come from Deborah; it came from within me. Working with her helped me look at my life in new ways that released my own energy and made it sing. I now choose my 'little battles' with faith and a happy heart." Here are Lily's new key aspirations and inspirations:

- I aspire to see with my heart into the hearts of those around me.
- I aspire to treat myself and others with love, respect, curiosity, compassion, and gratitude.
- I aspire to open myself to grace, letting it flow into and through me, guiding me through the day.
- I aspire to recognize the Divine design for me and be open to following the bread crumbs on my path.
- I aspire to finish this life in harmony with God and myself.

Viewing these aspirations and inspirations in terms of Abraham Maslow's famous hierarchy of needs, it is clear that Lily is functioning at the highest level, focusing on love, belonging, esteem, respect, creativity, and spirituality. Her life is an example of just how high you can climb, taking one baby step at a time, when you are willing to trust yourself and the Universe.

For more insights into embracing life's most difficult moments, read *The Way of Transition* by William Bridges.

The Lesson of Behave As If

The behave-as-if principle says that one potential way to create the new behaviors, environments, relationships, and feelings we want is to *behave as if* they were already present.

This approach goes much deeper than the popular "fake it till you make it" idea. If you give serious thought to how you would like your life to feel, a key component in making it a reality might be a specific set of characteristics and behaviors you would need to exhibit to make it happen. You might even find that those characteristics already exist as a cultural role model.

If, as Willie Nelson sings in his 1980 hit, your "heroes have always been cowboys" and you were trying to shape yourself into that ideal image, there are some things you might emulate and others you might avoid. For example, you might attend the rodeo, take horseback riding lessons, and wear flannel shirts, jeans, and boots. On the other hand, you probably wouldn't wear pink, eat tofu, or read *Oprah Magazine*.

Your cowboy role model would become a lens through which your choices would become obvious and well within your control. You could begin modifying your "packaging," skills, and actions to behave your way closer to how you'd like to feel and show up in life. As your external attributes begin to align with your ideal image, those initial successes would reinforce your belief that you *can* succeed, providing just the positive energy boost you may need to make it the rest of the way to achieving your ultimate goal.

My client Betty worked with me on using the behave-as-if principle to help her transform some of her self-sabotaging thought and behavior patterns. If you were to meet Betty, it would never occur to you that she was a person with confidence problems. She greets the world with a cheerful smile and the appearance of a solid professional, sure of her ability and her unique skill set.

The reality, however, is that she has a vision of how she'd like to show up in her life and she thus far feels that she hasn't been able to fit herself inside that particular skin.

When she considers why that is, Betty comes back to an idea that is all too common: she does a great job of taking care of, honoring, and watching over the other people in her life, but she herself falls far down on her priority list. In fact, if *she* wanted to be a cowboy, she probably wouldn't even make time to buy herself a pair of jeans. Meanwhile, she would make sure her children and clients had everything they needed to grow into their best selves.

Like so many of us, the great irony was that Betty didn't need an external role model after which to pattern her transition to her ideal image. The behaviors Betty desired were already well within her core strengths. It just wasn't occurring to her to apply them to meeting her own needs. In the words of Malcolm S. Forbes, "Too many people overvalue what they are not and undervalue what they are."

Using the behave-as-if principle can be a great way to get a new habit going and convince ourselves we have what it takes to go the distance. One of the ways she follows through on meeting the needs of her family and clients is to post reminder notes in places she can't miss. As a result of our work together, she has started posting notes all over her house reminding herself to notice and commit to meeting her needs and desires as well.

The benefits of learning to love herself have turned Betty into a strong advocate for this complex and rewarding work. "As a result of what I've learned in coaching with Deborah, I've engaged a colleague to serve as an 'accountability partner,'" she said. "I wanted a peer whose work is totally different from mine and who, like me, is willing to be held accountable and meet commitments not only to our clients and our families but to ourselves.

"Recently I started a newsletter for my clients. In the second issue, I talked about the importance of taking care of ourselves as well as we take care of everyone else in our lives. I shared my personal story with my clients, including the powerful return on investment I have received from investing my time, effort, and resources in working with a life coach. I know many of my clients will resonate with my story. My willingness to share it in an authentic way will likely open the door to even more powerful conversations between us."

As Elisabeth Kübler-Ross put it, "People are like stained-glass windows. They sparkle and shine when the sun is out, but when the darkness sets in their true beauty is revealed only if there is light from within."

A powerful way to turn on the light of love within you and keep it burning brightly is to ask yourself many times each day, "If I were my own beloved child or valued client, how would I take care of *me* right now?"

For more insights into recovering your authentic self and recognizing your vocation, read *Let Your Life Speak* by Parker J. Palmer.

Chapter 10:
Focus

With a firm energetic foundation and strong core in place, you are ready to leverage the insights from this chapter to focus your commitment to unconditional self-love so that you may go deeper and further on your Journey to Wholeness.

The Lesson of the Journey

Life is a journey, not a destination. We've heard it so often, we may be tempted to say, "Blah, blah, blah." But the lesson of the journey repeats so often in our language, literature, and culture that there must be more to it than first meets the eye.

The journey is the reward.

—The Tao

It is better to travel well than to arrive.

—Buddha

The good life is a process, not a state of being. It is a direction, not a destination.

—Carl Rogers

And you? When will you begin your long journey into yourself?

—Rumi, thirteenth-century Persian poet

You have brains in your head.
You have feet in your shoes.
You can steer yourself any direction you choose.
You're on your own, and you know what you know.
And you are the one who'll decide where you'll go.
                                        —Dr. Seuss

The consensus among thought leaders is that the journey itself should be valued, respected, and enjoyed. Why then do we so often behave like tourists on a cruise who choose to sleep whenever the ship is at sea, thinking that the things worth experiencing are only found at the "destinations?" In doing so, we miss the magnificent sunrises and the moonlit nights. The feeling of expansive possibilities as we gaze out on the seemingly endless ocean. The soft caress of the ocean breeze. How ironic that such "tourists" purchase trinkets at their "destinations" to remind them of a journey they missed.

Sam is a man who has always loved journeys. An avid cyclist, he had loved being physically active, but as he approached his sixtieth birthday, he began to feel that perhaps his best days were behind him. Even his bicycle, once a passion, now only served as a painful reminder that he wasn't quite as fast or as energetic as he used to be.

Although Sam remained in good health, he had reason to be increasingly aware of his own mortality: his dad had died young, and Sam saw aging as "mostly about loss." When he looked at people in their eighties and nineties, what he saw was the loss of energy, zest, and enthusiasm. When he looked in the mirror—or got on the scale—he saw the ten to fifteen pounds he had never carried before. The vision he saw ahead of himself was one of slow decline, increasing losses, and a deep sadness.

Sam first met me when he joined a life transitions group I facilitated. Moved by the possibilities for growth that he discovered in that group, he hired me as his personal life coach to help him sort out his feelings and create a more encouraging perspective on what lay ahead.

In our initial session, I asked him for a wish list—three things he would like to change about his life. His three items were closely related: more energy, the ability to continue being physically active as long as possible, and a powerful desire to ride his bike again.

Sam said he hadn't really been conscious of how long his bike had been gathering dust in the barn, but when he compared the life he wanted with the one he was living, his bike was a key indicator of what was missing. With his wish list in hand, we began addressing a wide range of topics in depth.

"While some people might have seen my fear of aging as 'normal' or 'to be expected' at my age, Deborah helped me to recognize that I was actually 'choosing' the very thing I feared the most every time I turned my back on the things I love," he said.

Whenever Sam walked away from his bike or the creative activities that fed his spirit by telling himself, "Fun doesn't matter," he took another step closer to the life he dreaded: a life of restricted activity and lower energy with a resigned and melancholy spirit. Every time he told himself his best days were behind him, he created a self-fulfilling prophecy.

Shortly after we began to coach together, Sam called me with a surprise to share: he and his wife had both gotten new bikes, gone on a three-day biking trip together, and spent the night at the top of Copper Mountain. Though he wasn't as fast as he once had been, he had loved every minute and knew his energy would increase as he got back in shape and continued letting go of his excess weight—physical, mental, emotional, and spiritual.

With a huge smile in his voice, Sam told me that his sixty-first summer had turned out to be one of the very best times of his life. He added that a friend in her late fifties also just got a new bicycle—a present from her husband to celebrate her new lease on life after hip replacement surgery. Sam sees clearly that they can both still be riding bikes and living the lives they love many years down the road.

Like many men, Sam doesn't wear his heart on his sleeve. Yet with the help of a supportive professional guide, he was able to connect with a part of himself that is deeply alive and filled with a passion for living. He says the ability to open that connection came, in large measure, from being respected and really listened to by his life coach.

Sam may never have heard Dr. Seuss's version of "The Lesson of the Journey," but he could easily add a few quotes on the subject himself!

For more insights into appreciating the joy of the journey, read _I Will Not Die an Unlived Life_ by Dawna Markova.

The Lesson of Living with Intention

Living with intention is often misunderstood as living with white-knuckle willpower and staying the course, even if "the course" was set by others or by a younger, less-experienced you.

Another common misconception is that living with intention means creating a to-do list every day and checking off your tasks as you complete them. While checking off a task on a list may yield a "yes" reaction and a sense of accomplishment, the benefit is momentary.

Neither is living with intention about superstition or even luck. The results you get from willpower, to-do lists, and luck are a poor substitute for the sense of abundance that comes from truly living with intention and mindfulness. My client Megan knows the real power of living with intention comes from within.

"This period has been the most stressful four years of my life," she said. "Not exactly a time when I stopped to smell the roses. Learning about mindfulness and about living with intention changed my life. We are so used to forcing things—issues, concerns, challenges—that it seems amazing when we allow them to surface organically. Just set the intention and put it out there, and it will surface in a way that is effortless and clear. Closest thing to magic that I know of."

Some people might find that a little "woo-woo" or New Age. Nothing could be further from the truth. Setting an intention and living mindfully are things anyone can do. No magic, quackery, or pseudoscience involved. The power of living with intention flows naturally from Albert Einstein's conclusion, based on his famous $e=mc^2$ equation, that everything is essentially energy, and from quantum physics principles that energy attracts like energy.

Conceptually, setting an intention is very different from setting goals. Setting an intention is not about a short- or long-term goal—something you will be _doing_ in the future. Instead, when you set your intention, you focus on how you are *being* in the present moment. Many have fully grasped the benefits of mindfulness and living with intention.

What lies behind us and what lies before us are tiny matters compared to what lies within us.
—*Oliver Wendell Holmes*

To embrace the wealth of the spirit, to revel in the wonders of life, to think, to remember, to dream—this is to know happiness.
—*Giancarlo di Gratsi*

Life loves to be taken by the lapel and told "I am with you, kid. Let's go."
—*Maya Angelou*

Megan uses mindfulness to stay tuned to her intentions. Instead of living with anxiety and obsessing over perfection, her three-step process is actually quite simple:

1. **Stop** what she's doing and address any gremlin voices demanding perfection.
2. **Check in** to see if she is functioning with compassion for herself and others or trying to bludgeon herself and others into doing things perfectly.
3. **Reaffirm** her intention.

Interestingly, Megan never set out to find a life coach, but synchronicity is a funny thing. The right thing happens at just the right time: a person you would love meeting appears, or a book you would love to read finds its way into your hands.

Synchronicity was at work the day Megan first called me. Having heard about me from one of her professional colleagues and long-time friends, she contacted me to see if our areas of expertise might lend themselves to some sort of collaboration. We began the process of discovery by learning about each other's work. That put

Megan in a sixty-minute complimentary coaching session with me, and the rest is history.

Megan's story is an amazing tale of transcendence and triumph. Over a period of four years, her life had become increasingly stressful. One challenge followed on the heels of another until she was drained, exhausted, angry, and sad—at risk for returning to the eating disorder she had beaten on her own years before.

Like many people, Megan easily steps into a caretaker role. Her approach to her profession was further enabling that behavior. If people needed help and were having a hard time, she would take on their energy and exhaust herself trying to fix it for them. One client in particular was "stuck" for nearly two years. Megan continued to support that client and others while pursuing a graduate degree in her spare time.

Meanwhile, Megan's beloved dog spent eighteen months having tumors removed, going through rehab, wearing braces, and generally feeling very sick. Someone else to care for.

Last but not least, Megan's family decided that this would be a good time to share some old family secrets with her. The conversation that ensued blew her idea of what her family was to smithereens. Idols fell, and her view of her personal world shifted.

"I had no idea how much I needed help. I hadn't realized how much I'd put my own needs on the shelf every day for the needs of others." As we worked together, Megan realized the harm she was doing to herself by not honoring or giving voice to the depth of her feelings about her situation. With a healthy dose of love, respect, curiosity, compassion, and gratitude, she finally got in touch with her feelings and began the painful but rewarding process of genuine communication.

In the process, Megan came to understand that we are all doing the best we can with the love and light we have at the time. Her relationships are healthier because her family understands what *she* is going through. She has taken them off a pedestal, preferring to build real, honest relationships instead.

"The most meaningful changes to result from this work come from four major shifts in my consciousness: (1) seeing myself clearly, (2) understanding, with grace, why I do what I do and how my personal board members show up in supportive and dysfunctional ways, (3) practicing mindfulness—being able to stop and be fully present in the space between a thought and my response, and (4) choosing my life rather than allowing it to be dictated by everyone and everything around me."

Megan followed a similar process when healing from her eating disorder. Through our work together, she realized those same core principles could be applied to any situation where she was allowing anxiety and perfectionism to taint her experience of life.

For more insights into living with intention, read *Live with Intention: Rediscovering What We Deeply Know* by Mary Anne Radmacher.

The Lesson of Connection

Imagine for a moment that you are a satellite. In the silence and the darkness of space, you regularly receive and transmit information to Earth. The communication works smoothly most of the time, and even if your signal is sometimes disrupted temporarily, the disruption rarely lasts very long.

You go on your way, secure in your orbit and in who and what you are. Until something happens to disrupt your orbit or positioning significantly. In space, it could be a blast of excess energy from the sun.

For a satellite that is turned away from its source, there is no option except to begin transmitting "Lost Earth" repeatedly, with no assurance the signal will ever be heard.

Those melancholy words, "Lost Earth," reflect disconnection from the only Source the satellite "knows."

Unlike a satellite, when something disrupts our "orbit" and connections to our Source, we might not even recognize that we are no longer communicating with our authentic self. In life, it could be a serious illness, a job loss, or just too many little challenges at one time. Unlike the satellite, our "programming" may keep us from crying out for help.

Over time, if the connection between how we show up in the world and who we are at our core becomes weaker and weaker, our personal orbit becomes askew, and only a significant repositioning can put us back in touch and back on track. Meanwhile—during the time of that disconnection—the darkness and the silence within can become as profound as the vast darkness and silence of outer space.

By now, you may be wondering what all this has to do with life coaching. When I met my client Cecilia, an expert in satellite technology, she described herself as having "Lost Earth." She realized that over a period of years she had faced away, or disconnected, from her authentic self. With her wry sense of humor, she wondered if anyone would notice or try to assist her if she walked around saying, "Lost Earth."

What does it look like when we disconnect from our essential, authentic selves? To an outside observer, it might look like life on a hamster wheel—busy, busy, busy. No longer spending time doing things we used to love, like music, art, or outdoor activities.

Those pastimes or passions slip away, quietly, slowly. We are stuck out there in the darkness and the silence. The external self has turned away and cannot see or "receive" from the authentic self any longer.

Cecilia didn't disconnect from her true self because of solar flares or solar wind. Instead, she disconnected for the same reasons many of us do: physical, mental, emotional, and spiritual burnout.

This kind of disconnection rarely happens overnight. It is more likely to creep up on us over time as life becomes increasingly complex. It might start with putting a spouse through law school and then dealing with marital problems, a divorce, a complex demanding job, and constant business travel. All of this continues until there is so little left of the authentic self and its many strengths that the next thing that comes along is just one thing too many. Staying connected to your authentic self is not just a nice thing to do. It is essential.

We shall not cease from exploration
And the end of all our exploring
Will be to arrive where we started
And know the place for the first time.

—*T.S. Eliot*

Your vision will become clear only when you can look into your heart. He who looks outside, only dreams, he who looks inside, also awakens.

—*Carl Jung*

In Cecilia's case, the one thing too many was becoming responsible for a father with multiple illnesses, including one that was slowly robbing him of his vision. As his health continued to decline, her responsibilities continued to escalate with exhausting complexity. Move him into assisted living. Deal with the realtors. Arrange for the sale of his house. Make sure his taxes were paid. Meet with his doctors. Make critical health care decisions.

At some point she made a conscious decision that she "didn't have time" for anything but work and her father. She consciously placed the things that brought her joy and were at the heart of her truest self on a back burner. She was just too busy to take care of herself too.

But even after her father died, nothing changed. She found herself still too busy, even though her responsibilities on his behalf had diminished to serving as executor of his estate. She was out of the real estate business and the health care business but was immersed instead in the business of wrapping up someone else's life.

By this time, she knew she needed help. She had worked with an iPEC life coach once before and knew that help was out there somewhere. One day she started actively looking. Her "Lost Earth" signal was going to be transmitted at last. In Cecilia's words, "I didn't want to talk about my feelings; I wanted to know what I could do to change my life." Having experienced an iPEC coach in the past, she started by researching coaches on iPEC's website. As it happened, I was their featured coach that day.

We connected through my life coaching website and set up a sixty-minute complimentary session. Our conversation revealed that we had more in common than living in Colorado. Many of the aspects of Cecilia's authentic self that had been left by the wayside were alive and well in me. A love of music, creative endeavors, and helping others provided a strong basis for connection between us. In the years leading up to my own burnout, I too had left them by the side of the road, too busy with work and taking care of everyone else to realize the long-term damage that would result.

As we worked together, Cecilia began to rebuild her own internal connections. Little by little, her "lost" self re-emerged. At her optometrist's office, she "happened" to notice the collection of ukuleles and asked about buying one and learning to play it.

"Life coaching gave me tools to help me navigate my life. When you have 'Lost Earth' and lost your way, what you need most is a new way to navigate." Once she got started, Cecilia learned to set her intention and tap into more and more of her authentic self. Beyond the rediscovery of her joy in music and quilting, she began looking seriously at what she'd like to do when she retires. How could she prepare? What might she bring to the next chapter of her life in light of all she had learned?

Today she has a business model and website that will help her assist other women in using creativity to deal with some of the challenges she has faced. She is fully engaged with a new vision of her future and has new tools to help her should she ever find that she has once again, even momentarily, "Lost Earth."

For more insights into finding lasting joy and fulfillment, read *The Ultimate Happiness Prescription* by Deepak Chopra.

Part IV:
Living the Lessons

If you have an unflinching commitment to knowing yourself better and doing the deep and rewarding work necessary, you will turn the life you dream of into a reality. When you show up with an unwavering passion for changing your life, a commitment to courageous self-exploration, and a willingness to try new ways of being, everything else will fall into place.

Everything we encounter is an opportunity to go backward, stay stuck, or move forward. It is up to you. When you choose constructive core energy centered in love, respect, curiosity, compassion, and gratitude, you change your experience to a generous, effortless, gracious life of flow filled with faith, hope, prosperity, peace, and joy. A life of freedom centered in being, not doing.

Chapter 11:
Finding a Guide

O ne of the most frequent questions I am asked is, "How long have you been doing this work?" My answer is, "Forever," because the purpose of life is making my own Journey to Wholeness and, through my journey, supporting others on their personal journeys as well. All of what we do here, things we call work and things we may label as rest or play, are meant to help us find our way back to the wholeness we once knew. All of my roles—artist, daughter, teacher, animal lover, author, sister, organization transformation consultant, wife, Reiki master, mother, spiritual celebrant, friend, life coach, and countless others—have been about making my journey while being a loving companion on the collective journey of all.

My clients inspire me every day with the certainty that all of us can take this Journey to Wholeness. Their stories are rooted in the safety and trust that come from a coaching relationship based on love, respect, curiosity, compassion, and gratitude.

The answers to the questions below will help you gain a better understanding of life coaching in order to appreciate the potential for life transformation, understand my approach, decide whether it's a modality that works for you, and begin to determine whether you and I might have the right chemistry as a team. I appreciate sharing in your journey through this book and look forward to the possibility of working with you more deeply by coaching together.

What is a professional life coach?
A professional life coach is a trusted, objective, nonjudgmental guide who provides a confidential and safe environment in which clients can

explore their challenges and opportunities. The coach's only agenda is the client's agenda—helping clients achieve their goals.

Why is life coaching so powerful?

The real power of coaching is in the relationship and the process. By listening and caring deeply, coaches help clients connect with their own inner wisdom concerning the way they would like to live and the best way to get there. They partner with clients in determining what is blocking them and how to release the hold those blocks have over them, unleashing the positive energy that will fuel them forward. By learning to live this process in every moment, clients can increase their own ability to identify and attain their deepest desires, dramatically and permanently.

I've done some therapy. Are we going to spend a lot of time rehashing my past again?

In general, coaches are not focused on the past, problems, or mental illness. In part, that is because coaches see everything as an opportunity. If in the process of exploring what is blocking you from moving forward in the way you would like we discover that your blocks have roots in the past, we will examine those roots. Our purpose for exploring the past will be to identify and remove any negative blocks—digging them out by the roots rather than lopping them off at the surface with superficial behavioral change—for faster, longer-lasting results. The coach's focus always remains on helping clients determine how to move from where they are to where they want to be, shifting from a life that is functional to one that is optimal.

How can a coach help me without firsthand knowledge of what I have experienced?

Professional coaches don't use their own experience as a model of success for clients. A professional coach's true expertise is in the coaching process, with specializations in a variety of fields. While they may share ideas from their own intuition, knowledge, and experience, they hold a deep belief that clients are the experts in their own lives and have within them optimal answers to any situations they face.

Through highly developed intuition and insightful questioning, a coach is a loving mirror that surfaces patterns and reflects them back to you to help you see new opportunities in yourself, your situations, and your relationships.

As a life coach, do you coach business situations?

Yes. I coach *everything* because *life* includes *everything*. I hold multiple professional coaching certifications, including board certification. I'm also retired from a thirty-year consulting career specializing in human resources and organization transformation, including serving as a senior partner in four of the world's largest and most prestigious global professional services firms. By virtue of my experience and expertise, I am well qualified to coach executives and professionals at all levels concerning a multitude of business situations.

Going beyond qualifications, the real answer is that life is just *life*. Despite our best efforts to separate our work and personal lives, those boundaries prove artificial, superficial, and highly permeable. Whether a client comes to me wanting help with a work situation or a personal relationship, inevitably the lines blur. Wherever you go, there you are. How you do anything is how you do everything. When you fall in love with yourself, everything else falls into place, *personally and professionally*. Choosing love as your core energy changes your perceptions, opportunities, relationships, and priorities. You release the illusion of separation and embrace the truth of oneness. When love transforms your relationship with yourself, *it can't help but transform your personal life, your work, and the world.*

What role does accountability play in working with a professional coach?

Accountability is not just valuable, it's essential. Professional coaches collaborate with their clients to develop and implement a plan of action to move them closer to their hearts' desires. They support clients in achieving rapid, extraordinary, sustainable results by partnering and holding them accountable for what they commit to doing. In my experience, this takes one of two forms:

1. Helping those who have difficulty holding themselves accountable to learn to do so with love and respect by creating a reasonable plan based on a series of achievable baby steps that will allow them to flow into completion.

2. Helping those who've been accountable for everyone and everything since birth learn to eliminate much of what is on their list and, with love and respect, replace it with a reasonable plan based on a series of achievable baby steps that includes rest, reflection, and play at the top of the list. We can give nothing of lasting value from an empty well.

What difference does coach certification make?

Certification substantiates coach training, experience, and credentials. Certified professional life coaches have received deep training through an accredited coach training program such as iPEC's. They have substantial experience across a broad range of coaching situations. They have been tested and are credentialed through independent professional organizations such as the International Coach Federation (ICF) and the Center for Credentialing and Education (CCE).

Why is more than 90 percent of life coaching done by phone rather than in person?

There are many reasons why coaches and their clients prefer coaching by phone rather than in person:

- **Ideal coach match:** Because you are not limited by geographic proximity, you have greater ability to choose the coach with the best style, specialty, credentials, and references, providing the opportunity for an ideal match to your needs and personality.
- **Flexible and convenient:** The coach and client can be anywhere they choose. Given today's busy lifestyles, it is a great benefit for both of us not to need to show up physically at the same place and time.

- **Efficient and affordable:** Coaching by phone lowers overhead costs, eliminates travel time, and reduces fossil fuel consumption.
- **Relaxing and confidential:** Because you choose where and when to take your coaching call, no one needs to know who you are talking with or about what.
- **Effective:** With a highly intuitive, well-credentialed, extensively experienced professional life coach, coaching by phone is often more effective than meeting in person. With the removal of potential distractions from physical surroundings and personal reactions, experience demonstrates time and again that a coach's well-honed intuitive skills can support your discovery of insights that you might not reach as quickly or at all via in-person coaching.

There are only so many hours in a day. How do you decide which clients to work with?

I have one requirement—an unflinching commitment to knowing yourself better and doing the deep and rewarding work necessary to make the life you dream of a reality. If you show up with an unwavering passion for changing your life, a commitment to courageous self-exploration, and a willingness to try new ways of being, the rest of the details—format, timing, and fees—will sort themselves out.

Why do you base your coaching on iPEC's Energy Leadership model?

Energy Leadership delivers life-transforming results. Energy Leadership refers to the process of leading your energy so it works for you rather than against you. By learning and applying the principles and concepts of Energy Leadership, you can increase your ability to shift your own energy and the energy of those around you. When you do that, you will help inspire and motivate yourself and others, feel a greater sense of purpose, and get more done with much less effort and stress.

How does completing the Energy Leadership Index assessment support your clients' growth?

The Energy Leadership Index assessment, or ELI, is a life attitude assessment based on an energy/action model. It reveals how the thoughts, emotions, and behaviors you choose are affecting the energy you live with in every moment, which in turn affects the results you get. It measures your level of energy based on your attitude—your perception of and perspective on your world. Because attitude is subjective, it is also malleable. By working with an Energy Leadership master practitioner coach and the ELI, you can alter your attitude, change your perspective, shift your consciousness, increase your energy, and enhance your leadership effectiveness, personally and professionally.

I'm still not sure coaching is for me. How can I be sure?

Sign up for a no obligation complimentary coaching session. If someone offered you a precious gift for an hour of your time, would you be interested? That is what I offer with a complimentary coaching session. A comp session isn't a brief demo or sample. It is a full forty-five-minute coaching session focused on current real-life challenges of your choosing plus fifteen minutes to discuss your experience and any questions you may have about my approach to coaching.

Those who have experienced comp sessions will tell you, when you come to your session open to the possibilities for transformation and fully committed to your own growth, big breakthroughs happen! I believe so deeply in the benefits of a complimentary session that I require them before entering into any individual coaching relationship. My clients and I find this up-front investment of our energy provides the firmest foundation for our work together. Actually coaching together is one of the best ways to appreciate the potential for life transformation, understand my approach, decide whether it is a modality that works for you, and determine whether you and I have the right chemistry as a team.

Chapter 12:
Supporting Your Success

H aving read this book and explored the insights, you may be wondering how you too can learn to *live* the lessons— turning them into a new, less stressful, more fulfilling way of life. This book may have provided some glimpses into new possibilities and raised as many new questions as it answered.

Everything we encounter is an opportunity to go backward, stay stuck, or move forward. To support yourself in continuing to move forward with the life lessons shared in this book, I invite you to scan the QR code to the right or visit www. tiny.cc/djwbookclub to **join my Book Insider Club** for *free*. As a member, you will receive periodic updates on book signings and events, as well as exclusive access to expanded book content and special book purchase promotions, including the opportunity to buy the companion workbooks and other related resources to support you on your personal Journey to Wholeness.

Here are some of the tools, resources, and programs available to you online through my coaching, social media, and Internet talk radio sites:

- Broaden your perspective. Visit www.tiny.cc/djwbookclub to **download large, full-color illustrations**, including all of the charts in the book and other inspiring images to support your personal journey.
- Give your energy an added boost. Visit www.tiny.cc/djwradio to **tune into my weekly Internet talk radio show**, *Choose Your Energy: Change Your Life*, airing globally on the EmPOWERment Channel of VoiceAmerica. Visit

www.tiny.cc/djwradioarchive to **browse My Radio Show Archive** with excerpts of all past episodes and access to full recordings.

- **Join my Radio Show Insider Club** for *free* at www.tiny. cc/djwradioclub. As a member, you will receive periodic updates on upcoming programs and guest cohosts, as well as exclusive promotional offers, access to the latest show recordings, and other bonus content.
- **Subscribe to my monthly newsletter,** including unlimited archive access to past volumes, at www.tiny.cc/djwnews.
- **Follow my blog** at www.tiny.cc/djwblog. Stay on top of the latest inspirational installments by signing up for email notification when new blogs post each week.
- **Access my other social media sites** at www.tiny.cc/ djwsocialmedia for additional *free* life-affirming content.
- **Visit my one-stop shop** at www.tiny.cc/djwoffers for easy access to everything I offer, plus links to trusted third-party providers.
- Experience the transformational power of learning to love yourself unconditionally by **scheduling a complimentary coaching session** at www.tiny.cc/djwcompsession. The value of a comp session? *Priceless!*
- Begin applying these powerful tools and techniques to transform your own life. **Purchase an individual or group coaching program** at www.tiny.cc/djwprograms.
- I am always posting new insights and information on my main coaching website. Visit www.djwlifecoach.com often to **expand your possibilities**.

By creating a life worth living, you learn the art of living—enjoying the journey. Your own life is your greatest creative work. Begin the exciting journey of falling in love with yourself. Today is neither too soon nor too late!

About the Author

If you've ever had the opportunity to watch someone grow in a completely extraordinary way, you will understand what friends and clients mean when they say they love the very "idea" of Deborah.

Starting her professional career as an organization transformation consultant in 1975, over the next thirty years, Deborah went on to serve as a senior partner in four of the world's largest and most prestigious global professional services firms.

Despite her positions and fancy titles, people at all levels were drawn to her. While the windup toys on her desk and the rubber chicken hanging from her ceiling may have engaged everyone's curiosity, it was her combination of piercing intellect, good humor, and playfulness that put people at ease.

Deborah had some wonderful times in that thirty-year career. She coached, taught, and encouraged clients and colleagues to claim their personal power and step into their greatness. But three decades on the "hamster wheel" with little regard for her personal health and welfare took their toll. She retired in 2005, a poster child for professional burnout: exhausted, morbidly obese, and clinically depressed.

In 2008 and 2009, Deborah hit bottom. She lost three loved ones in five weeks and found herself living alone for the first time in her life when her husband of seventeen years took an important assignment in Washington, DC. That "alone time" became a crucible in which Deborah transformed herself physically, mentally, emotionally, and spiritually. In the process, she discovered that when she fell in love with herself, everything else in her life finally fell into place. She transformed her existence and found her purpose as a life coach and Reiki master, guiding others on their Journeys to Wholeness.

Through her writing, speaking, radio show, and signature coaching programs, Deborah helps individuals and organizations harness the transformative power of love to step into their greatness.

For fun, Deborah loves singing, reading, sewing, and movies. She currently lives in Aurora, Colorado, with her husband, Wilson, and the three coaching cats who manage her life—SiddhaLee, Mortimer, and Maisy Jane.

To learn more about the life-transforming power of falling in love with yourself, explore Deborah's website at www.djwlifecoach.com, subscribe to her blog at www.tiny.cc/djwblog, and listen to her weekly Internet talk radio show at www.tiny.cc/djwradio.

Appendix

Meditation

I am in the Deepak Chopra "WW" camp: Whatever Works. It doesn't have to take thirty minutes in an uncomfortable posture in a darkened room, chanting "Om" to center yourself. While, intense, lengthy meditation can be a wonderful experience, in the real world, I find the time I most need the effects of a meditative recentering are the very times when it's not realistic to take a prolonged break.

For example, I get an unexpected call from the IRS agent handling my audit. It would be great if I had a real-time way to bring myself back to center while remaining in constructive conversation with him. It might not enhance the credibility of my case if I say, "Excuse me, sir. You are freaking me out so much I'm on the verge of hyperventilating. I'm sure you'll understand that I simply must hang up so I can go sit alone in a small darkened room for thirty minutes before continuing this discussion any further." In a crisis, it might come to that, but I prefer to have some tools I can call on in the moment before resorting to hiding in my bedroom closet.

Real-time meditation can be as simple as closing your eyes and taking a single intentional breath while repeating in your head a phrase that centers you: I am healthy, happy, and whole. My Source is excellent, limitless, and reliable. I choose love and abundance. I know *who* I am and *Whose I am*. Experiment to find your personal array of WW on-the-spot meditation mantras.

Anything can be a meditation when approached with mindfulness and the intention to clear yourself of fear, recenter, and open yourself wide as a conduit for love and light—raking leaves, walking the dog, drying dishes, scooping cat litter, washing the car, folding laundry, cleaning floors.

Some like to set reminders on their cellphones or computers to chime every hour and remind them to stop and take their intentional breath. Others observe daily morning and bedtime gratitude practices. As soon as they open their eyes in the morning and just before closing them again at night, they "bookend" their day by naming at least five things they are grateful for. Some days it is a struggle to name five. The list looks like, "Air to breath, water to drink, my cat, my dog, my bed." Other days the list goes on forever. Fostering an attitude of gratitude is one of the best ways to foster a life of flow.

Some people observe the "breath of celebration" ritual. Before turning to the next task, they stop and take a breath of gratitude and celebration for what they just accomplished. This habit proved especially useful for me while writing this book. Whatever the size of the task completed, the perfect word or a new ten-page chapter, all were worthy of celebration. Anything worthwhile and monumental is accomplished one baby step at a time. The joy generated by sixty seconds of celebrating will provide the constructive fuel to help you flow right on into the next task. You will find yourself much less stressed and much more productive.

One of my favorite "meditation" practices was originally inspired by Julia Cameron's "morning pages" journaling technique. Over a period of months, my three-a-day morning pages broadened into a substantive written meditation practice in which I reflected upon the writings of my ever-expanding group of spiritual elders. Each day I read a bit from three to five different inspiring writers and then contemplate how their words that particular day show up in my life: who I am and whatever I'm wrestling with at the moment. Some days I wake up and just start writing. When I'm all written out, I read a bit from each of my elders and write more if I feel the call. Other days I read a bit from the first elder and then write a bit, read from the next and write a bit more, read from another and write some more; this continues until I feel grounded and have set my intentions for the day.

The process sounds simple. The result is profound. I joke that the authors of my various daily readings books stay up each night creating the next day's meditations just for me, because the alignment of their messages with the specific demands of each day is nothing short of miraculous.

This written practice has become a core tool in recognizing imbalances, analyzing root causes, and identifying the necessary physical, mental, emotional, and spiritual adjustments needed to return me to wholeness. Key to the nutritional aspect of my lifestyle, when I recognize the urge to eat though I am not physically hungry, even if it is raw veggies with negligible calories, my only rule is that I always get real with myself. Sometimes I start with the question, "Would God be eating this right now? Or would God realize a lack of food is not the issue?" Then I stop and write until I identify the real void I am trying to fill or emotion I am trying to smother. If after getting to the heart of the matter I still want to eat three pounds of carrots in one sitting, no problem. As long as I am also working on the real issue as well.

Many spiritual teachers offer great guided meditation programs. For example, four times a year, through The Chopra Center, Deepak Chopra offers a new, completely free, series of twenty-one daily guided meditations organized around a central theme (love, abundance, health, etc.). I love the programs in this series and use them myself. He even offers the opportunity to purchase the complete set of meditations on CD or via download so you can benefit from including them in your ongoing practice. I own eight different Chopra programs, plus four collections of his meditation music, mantras, and "greatest hits." I rotate through the programs on a regular basis, using them to expand, enrich, and diversify my meditative options. The daily sessions are simple web-accessible recordings lasting ten to twenty minutes each. For many of my clients who wanted to enjoy the benefits of regular meditation but just couldn't make it happen, embracing this program has been the key to establishing a consistent practice.

Whether you are an experienced meditator or have heard that it might reduce your stress, improve your creativity, and increase your sense of well-being, this program has a great deal to offer. It's based on the findings that it takes twenty-one days to change or create a habit. For those new to meditation, it eliminates the perceived barrier of "too much silence" by easing you into a healthy new habit through a theme that ties the twenty-one sessions together with lots of teaching, guidance, and music. For the seasoned meditator, it's a great way to expand your options and approach. All meditation paths have merit because at their core they all are about the myriad ways we can foster mindfulness. Doing the dishes, walking the dog, feeding the cat—all become meditative when entered into with focus and awareness. We are human beings *not* human doings. Just me, just here, just now, just be. To learn more about the Chopra programs, visit www.chopracentermeditation.com.

Tonglen

One of the things I love about Tonglen meditation is that instead of the common approach of breathing in the "good" and breathing out the "bad," Tonglen works in reverse. Here is my personal adaptation of the Tonglen process I learned from Pema Chödrön.

Starting with the principle that fear is the author of lies and illusion while love is the author of truth and reality, breathe in as deeply and fully as you possibly can the very worst version you can imagine of whatever you're fearing. As you do, imagine a bubble of illusion growing larger and larger filled with that particular fear-based lie. When your lungs have expanded to the limit, hold your breath for a few seconds while setting your intention to release the lie of the illusion based in fear and replace it with the truth of a reality based in love.

Having set your intention, reach out and gently pop the bubble of fear filled with lies and reveal it for the illusion it always is. As you do so, exhale for everyone and everything in the Universe your new reality of love-based truth. All fear has been fully replaced by love. Repeat as many cycles of inhale, transform, and exhale as you need to begin feeling yourself recenter. On the final release, see yourself at the center of a reality based in the truth of love with everyone and everything in the Universe in perfect order within and around you.

It can be helpful to recite in your head a three-part mantra as you go, for example:

- (*Inhale*) I breathe in the fear and scarcity of my relationship with my boss. I breathe it in for myself. I breathe it in for my boss. I breathe it in for everyone who has ever felt this pain.

- I recognize this feeling as an illusion filled with fear-based lies. (*Pop*)
- (*Exhale*) I breathe out the Universal truth of love and abundance in this and all relationships, for myself and everyone, everywhere, and at all times.

When you choose your energy, you can change your life and the lives of everyone and everything you encounter. You set in motion a ripple effect of constructive energy fueled by love and possibilities.

As promised in the chapter 5 exploration of the sense of creativity, here is blog post concerning Tonglen that resulted from my blog writing frustration on the final day of my short-lived sister blog site, "*Love and Curiosity: Gems for the Journey.*"

I had spent much of the previous two days listening to eight Chödrön lectures on Tonglen meditation. Throughout the program, she warned that the more you study and practice meditation, the more you will encounter your own frustrating nature. Just when you think you should have it all together, you realize the only thing you've figured out is that you don't have it all together. Everything was just ducky that day until I sat down to write my newest blog post. Then the whining began. Bingo!

I used to think meditators were people who had risen above normal human experience. They were always very Zen—chanting and not caring about anything. Boy, was I clueless. According to Chödrön, meditation isn't about escaping your emotions; it's about embracing them—the good, the bad, and the ugly. It's about awakening your heart with constant awareness of yourself and your feelings. It's about observing them with love and curiosity and accepting everything about yourself, especially the most frustrating aspects. The point of enlightenment is not to become superior and feel no pain. It's to open your heart wider to your own pain and, through that experience, to the pain of others. It's to help you develop deeper love and true empathy for yourself and everyone else so you can finally connect to all of humankind on the most profound level by understanding we are one.

So there I sat. Tired, confused, not sure where my life was headed. Feeling a little sorry for myself. Annoyed that I'd committed myself to a second blog site. Not sure what to write that would inspire anyone else when I felt so uninspired. Not sure anyone really cared whether I wrote then or ever. Nothing to write. No reason to write. So alone.

In tears of frustration, I closed my eyes, started breathing slowly and deeply, and asked for guidance. The answer came: "Observe the teachings of Tonglen."

- (*Inhale*) I embrace the misery I am creating for myself.
- (*Exhale*) With compassion, I send myself love, joy, and peace.
- (*Inhale*) I focus on the people all over the world who are tired and confused.
- (*Exhale*) Others who don't know if they are on the right path.
- (*Inhale*) Others who feel alone and that no one cares.
- (*Exhale*) With compassion, I send them love, joy, and peace.

After a few cycles of breathing and holding these thoughts, peace enveloped me. I knew that all over the world, others were observing their own version of this practice or another form of prayer or meditation as they sat with their own personal pain. We were total strangers and yet we were thinking of each other with compassion and sending each other love, joy, and peace. We were not alone. Someone did care. We cared. For me, that's Tonglen meditation in a nutshell.

Daily Practice

After completing my morning written meditation, I close with my daily practice, during which I clear myself of all fear, realign my energy and intentions, and dedicate myself as a clear channel for love and light, with the commitment to learn my lessons quickly and gently and help others do so as well. This practice is my daily rededication to the truth that, when I am free of all fear and aligned with love as my Source, my very presence raises the constructive energy of every being and situation I encounter. Because I am a Reiki master, my practice includes affirmations based on the core intentions of the Reiki symbols. I share it to inspire you to develop your own personalized daily practice through which you clear yourself of fear, realign yourself with love, embrace your truths, and dedicate yourself to your personal path.

The first phase of my daily practice is a centering process I use with my clients at the beginning of each coaching session. It can be used on its own anytime you are feeling stressed or scattered and wish to recenter yourself. I sit comfortably, close my eyes, and begin breathing slowly and deeply just focusing on my breath. I then imagine gathering up all the aspects of myself that I might have left strewn across the landscape of my day, embracing and honoring all of them as I continue breathing and settling in. Then, knowing that it is neither loving nor useful to carry everything in my immediate consciousness at every moment, I notice whether anything from my *past* is distracting me or hooking my energy in a way that is blocking my ability to be fully here now. If so, I take my *left hand* and lift off those elements with love and respect, parking them on an imaginary shelf in space just over my *left shoulder*. I'm not rejecting any part of my experience, merely choosing what positions me best for centering in this moment. If I need to access any of the things I've "parked" during the meditative practice, they will be easily available to me from that location. Carrying them right now is neither kind nor helpful. I continue breathing, recognizing that I already feel somewhat lighter and clearer. I then notice whether anything from my *future* is distracting me or hooking my energy in a way that is blocking my ability to be fully here now. If so, I take my *right hand* and lift off those elements with love and respect, parking them on an imaginary shelf in space just over my *right shoulder*. I'm not rejecting any part of my experience, merely choosing what positions me best for centering in this moment. If I need to access any of the things I've "parked" during the meditative practice, they will be easily available to me from that location. Carrying them right now is neither kind nor helpful. I continue breathing, recognizing that I feel even lighter and clearer, with unfettered access to my deepest insights and discernment.

I then shift into the second phase of my daily practice. The first sixteen steps and two of the final three steps of this phase include drawing the respective Reiki symbols in the air while reciting the phrases they embody for me and placing my hands briefly on the relevant chakra or combination of chakras. The names of the respective symbols appear in parentheses after each affirmation. I do most of the "reciting," whether phrases or sentences, in my head. When an area needs extra attention, I will say it aloud and repeat it until I feel the tension I'm carrying start to release and my energy realigns with a more constructive frequency. You don't need to *be* a Reiki master or do the practice *with* a Reiki master for it to have meaning. Just focus your energy on the intentions of the affirmations. They flow from Universal truths espoused by many spiritual traditions that anyone may benefit from embracing.

The remaining affirmations are based on ones I learned from my spiritual elders and others I came up with on my own. You may recognize in the list my versions of the Shambhala *Four Limitless Ones* affirmations, don Miguel Ruiz's *Five Agreements*, Marianne Williamson's *Five Principles of Everyday Grace*, and Master Teacher Usui Mikao's *Five Reiki Ideals*. Yes, I memorized the complete practice over time. It started out with my two core personal affirmations and grew as I identified additional intentions that bolstered my particular energetic susceptibilities and my level of Reiki practice advanced from novice to Karuna Master. The list is dynamic; during the launch of my weekly talk radio show and writing of this book, I added the affirmations about sensory balance and renewal. Given my history, it's unsurprising that those aspects of my life might have warranted additional *attention* and *intention* to keep me centered during such big new endeavors. Here is the essence of my daily practice.

- I detach and clear (Jakikiri Jokaho Kenyoku).
- I greet the Divine (Zonar).
- I embrace Divine power (Choku Rei).
- I transcend time and space (Hon Sha Ze Sho Nen).
- I open my heart wide (Tibetan Dai Ko Mio).
- I restore equanimity (Sei Heki).
- I heal myself (Halu).
- I heal my relationships (Harth).
- I blanket all with love (Usui Dai Ko Myo).
- I align my energy (Ra Ku Kei).

- I connect with Divine mind (Gnosa).
- I honor boundaries (Iava).
- I embrace oneness (Om).
- I embody peace (Shanti).
- I manifest the highest good (Kriya).
- I anchor my intentions (Rama).
- I do not worry. I am grateful and faithful.
- I am not angry or impatient. I am generous, kind, and compassionate. We are each doing our best with the love and light we have at the time.
- I am impeccable with my word. I do not use it to injure or deceive myself or others.
- I take nothing personally. I respect that we are each on our own path doing our own personal work.
- I make no assumptions. The Universe is far greater than I can imagine, even on my most brilliant day.
- I listen deeply and with discernment. I always trust my intuition and inner wisdom.
- I always do my best with the love and light I have at the time.
- Miracles happen.
- We do the work of the angels.
- I do not judge. Judging blocks the light.
- I hold myself in alignment with the highest good.
- Sacred silence rights the Universe.
- I enjoy loving-kindness and fostering loving-kindness.
- I am free from misery and fostering misery.
- I choose joy.
- I dwell in equanimity, free from craving, aversion, and indifference.
- I do not rush. I am enough. I discern, focus, and follow through. The Universe works wonders through me.
- I live in harmony, encouraging sensory balance through mindfulness, wisdom, and love.
- I do not give from an empty well. I renew and empower my body, mind, heart, and soul with rest, reflection, and play.
- I approach life with love, respect, curiosity, and compassion, revealing and advancing the highest good.
- My gratitude for Universal abundance anchors each moment

in generous, effortless, gracious flow filled with faith, hope, prosperity, peace, and joy.

- Whatever my circumstances, I know *who* I am and *Whose* I am: a unique cocreative expression of the Divine.
- I free myself of all fear and dedicate myself as a clear channel for love and light. I learn my lessons quickly and gently and help others do so as well.
- I love You. I hold Your hand. I walk in Your path.
- You are my Source: excellent, limitless, and reliable. No external force can block my highest good. Universal abundance flows to and through me.
- I consecrate my thoughts, words, and deeds. I open my heart for the highest good. Blessed be all through me.
- I detach and clear (Jakikiri Jokaho Kenyoku).
- I seal with Divine power (Choku Rei).
- I am loved and loving, blessed and a blessing. And so it is. Namaste. Amen.

Statement of Intentions

To help me gain greater clarity concerning what it means when I affirm that I know *who* I am and *Whose* I am, I developed a highly personal statement of intentions based on my values and purpose. I share it to inspire you to develop your own intentions based on your values and purpose. My statement is posted over my desk, in my kitchen, and next to the bathroom mirror—places where I tend to linger over tasks and benefit from the opportunity to remind myself of my core beliefs and motivations. In particularly stressful situations, I recite a relevant item from the list. Other times I read the entire list aloud as an overall reminder. I encourage you to experiment with developing your own deeply meaningful intentions and ways of using them to support you on your Journey to Wholeness.

- I love myself. I am healthy, happy, and whole, at peace living a life I love, and enjoying deep and meaningful relationships with others.
- Every minute of every day, I hold my heart and mind wide

open. I pay attention. I do the work. I walk the talk. I provide the centering and nurturing to support my growth.

- I empower my healing with mindfulness, love, wisdom, and commitment.
- I am a liberator. Through my work as an inspirational writer, speaker, healer, and coach, I help countless people learn to love themselves, foster constructive energy, and manifest meaning-filled lives.
- When I hold myself in alignment with the highest good as a clear channel for love and light, the Universe works wonders through me.
- I have everything to manifest the life I dream of.
- My prosperity is firmly grounded in trusting my intuition, energy, and discernment regarding what, why, when, and how.
- In all I dream and do, I am a unique cocreative expression of the Divine, fostering balance, harmony, and understanding.
- I release my intentions and desires to the Universe to help me manifest in the specific ways that will best support the highest good for all, in all, through all.

Spiritual Elders

In a spirit of gratitude, I want to take a minute to share the names of the elders who have been instrumental in shaping my insights and personal growth to date:

- As I already shared in the chapter 5 exploration of the inner sense of creativity, Julia Cameron has had a profound impact on my life. Through her teachings, I saved and transformed my life by understanding that creativity is not optional, it's essential; that a life infused with creativity is one of power, joy, and endless possibilities; that God is my Source and the origin of all creativity; and that the essence of God's relationship with me is unconditional love, not fear.
- Pema Chödrön's writings have changed the way I experience everyone and everything. They have expanded my ability to truly empathize with myself and others by judging less

and unconditionally loving more. Her Tonglen real-time meditation approach has become a way of life.

- Caroline Myss has served as the queen of tough love in my life. Back in the mid-1990s, her work on the interconnection of body, mind, heart, and soul laid the foundation for the physical, mental, emotional, and spiritual transformation I would undergo more than ten years later. As a life coach, I have also benefitted greatly from her newer books, particularly *Sacred Contracts* and the deeply personal role archetypes play in the habitual light and shadow aspects of our thoughts, feelings, and behavior. Embracing those teachings has been like getting a PhD in what is often referred to as personality theory, broadening and deepening my understanding of the inner drivers and transformation opportunities for myself and my clients.

- Albert Ellis's classic book on rational emotive therapy, *A Guide to Rational Living,* was the core text for my earliest experience with psychotherapy. He was the first writer to help me understand that our feelings and behaviors are driven by how we think and that we have the power to change how we feel and behave by changing how we think.

- Alice Miller's book *The Drama of the Gifted Child* was another core text from my early years in psychotherapy. I began to heal some of my oldest wounds with her insight that in order to heal any pain, I needed to first allow myself to feel the depth of it in a way I hadn't allowed myself to do at the time.

- William Bridges's work on transitions, most especially his book *The Way of Transition,* proved invaluable in understanding the role of the void/transition time and the downside of trying to cut it short. Appreciating that while it appears nothing is happening in the void, in fact everything is happening to incubate the new birth in the next period of life.

- Sue Monk Kidd's work on the Divine feminine and the benefits of time in the chrysalis was instrumental to my own self-discovery and personal growth and to supporting my clients on their Journeys to Wholeness.

- Thomas Moore's work on the role of soul in our lives and work was eye-opening and encouraging. In *Writing in the Sand* and other books he has authored, he helped me learn to differentiate the authentic core messages of Universal love shared by the world's great spiritual masters from the all-too-human religious attitudes that are fostered by fear.
- Parker J. Palmer's work on the importance of aligning soul and role, the power of nonjudgmental listening, and the truth that each of us has an inner guide supported my personal healing and shaped much of my approach to life coaching.
- Dawna Markova's penetrating questions and profound insights on living life to the fullest inspired me to ask myself and others the big questions.
- Oriah Mountain Dreamer taught me to appreciate the role of creativity in living a life that is fully and authentically my own.
- Mary Oliver's poignant poetry, most memorably "Wild Geese" and "The Journey" spoke to me of the importance of knowing, being, and taking care of myself.
- Wayne Muller helped me appreciate the spiritual advantages of a painful childhood and the role that rest and balance play in helping me keep a healthy perspective on who I am and where I have been. He reminded me that I am a human *being* not a human *doing* and that rest is an essential component of the fuel I use to empower myself to fulfill my purpose.
- Mary Anne Radmacher's writings challenged me to live with intention and on purpose.
- Louise L. Hay's teachings on the power of positive affirmations offered me a core tool for aligning my energy with my priorities to manifest the life I dream of.
- James Hillman's refreshing retake on classical psychology to incorporate the roles of soul and spirit into considerations of life purpose and calling reinforced my personal beliefs on the subject.
- Psychologist and art therapist Peter London reframed art, not as pleasing decoration but as deep spiritual practice and communication. He strengthened my belief that art is the way we tell our stories, the way we share what must be shared.

- I am encouraged and affirmed in my beliefs around balanced feeding of our nine senses by Cheryl Richardson's ideas on extreme self-care, which I encountered after I was well along my path of transformation through more balanced living. Her thoughts on grace and gratitude also resonated deeply with me.
- I could go on for weeks about Dr. Wayne W. Dyer. Top of mind and heart for me are his ability to bring to life with power, compassion, humor, and love the Tao, the prayer of St. Francis, the practice of mindfulness, and the fact that we choose the reality we create for ourselves. Bless you forever for giving me the question, "Which thought moves you forward?"
- Richard Brodie provoked my curiosity with his compelling concept that memes are essentially viruses of the mind. He reminded me that, because I choose my reality, I can also choose to think, feel, and behave differently.
- Bruce Lipton expanded my perspective with his work on the biology of belief and the power of consciousness. DNA is not an immutable prison sentence. I can change my DNA via the energetic messages of my thoughts, whether constructive or destructive.
- I love Gregg Braden's contention that a field of intelligence is encoded in our DNA and permeates all creation. I find especially intriguing his teaching that this field of intelligence is continually communicating with us about ourselves in each moment through an architecture based on seven mirrors of relationship identified by the ancient Essenes: (1) who we are; (2) what we judge; (3) what has been lost, given away, or taken away; (4) our most forgotten love; (5) our relationship with God; (6) our dark night of the soul; and (7) our perfection.
- Dr. Christiane Northrup and Dr. Mona Lisa Schulz taught me how to use my body's unique intuitive language to heal myself on the physical, mental, emotional, and spiritual levels.
- Marianne Williamson touched me deeply with a line from her famous poem, "Our deepest fear is not that we are inadequate. Our deepest fear is that we are powerful beyond

measure. It is our light, not our darkness that most frightens us" (1992). So true, so true.

- Shakti Gawain helped me understand that true prosperity is a spiritual, not financial, state. It is a frame of heart and mind. We choose whether to live limited lives or to embrace the unbelievable abundance the Universe offers in all ways, on all levels, at all times.

- Sonia Choquette helped me strengthen my intuition to partner more deeply with myself, my Divine Source, my clients, and all of creation.

- Deepak Chopra encouraged me along my chosen path with his teaching that our bodies are essentially energy and information and that mind and body are inseparable. Our awareness—beliefs, thoughts, and emotions—creates our biochemistry. Because our bodies and our world are defined by how we choose to perceive them, if we choose to change our beliefs, thoughts, and emotions, we change how we experience our bodies and our world. We are the observers, not victims, of our lives because we choose what to perceive.

References and Recommended Reading

H ere are some great reads that I cited or that provide additional insights to support you in deeper consideration and implementation of the topics explored in this book:

Breathnach, Sarah Ban. 1995. *Simple Abundance.* New York: Warner Books, Inc.

Braden, Gregg. 2005. *Awakening the Power of a Modern God.* Carlsbad: Hay House Audio.

Bridges, William. 1980. *Transitions.* Reading: Addison-Wesley Publishing Company, Inc.

———. 2001. *The Way of Transition.* Cambridge: Perseus Publishing.

Brodie, Richard. 1996. *Virus of the Mind.* Carlsbad: Hay House, Inc.

Brown, Brené. 2007. *I Thought It Was Just Me.* New York: Gotham Books.

———. 2010. *The Gifts of Imperfection.* Center City: Hazelden.

Cameron, Julia. 1996. *The Vein of Gold.* New York: Jeffery P. Tarcher/ Putnam.

Cameron, Julia. 2000. *God Is No Laughing Matter.* New York: Jeffery P. Tarcher/Putnam.

———. 2002. *The Artist's Way*. New York: Jeffery P. Tarcher/ Putnam.

———. 2002. *Walking in This World*. New York: Jeffery P. Tarcher/ Penguin.

———. 2006. *Finding Water*. New York: Jeffery P. Tarcher/ Penguin.

———. 2009. *The Artist's Way Every Day*. New York: Jeffery P. Tarcher/Penguin.

Chödrön, Pema. 1994. *Start Where You Are*. Boston: Shambhala Publications, Inc.

———. 2001. *The Places That Scare You*. Boston: Shambhala Publications, Inc.

———. 2002. *Comfortable With Uncertainty*. Boston: Shambhala Publications, Inc.

Chopra, Deepak. 1993. *Ageless Body, Timeless Mind*. New York: Three Rivers Press.

———. 2009. *The Ultimate Happiness Prescription*. New York: Harmony Books.

Choquette, Sonia.1994. *The Psychic Pathway*. New York: Crown Trade Paperbacks.

———. 1997. *Your Heart's Desire*. New York: Three Rivers Press.

———. 2000. *True Balance*. New York: Three Rivers Press.

Dreamer, Oriah Mountain. 1999. *The Invitation*. San Francisco: HarperSanFrancisco.

———. 2001. *The Dance*. San Francisco: HarperSanFrancisco.

———. 2002. *Your Heart's Prayer*. Boulder: Sounds True, Incorporated.

———. 2003. *The Call*. San Francisco: HarperSanFrancisco.

————. 2005. *What We Ache For*. San Francisco: HarperSanFrancisco.

Dyer, Dr. Wayne W. 2004. *101 Ways to Transform Your Life*. Carlsbad: Hay House, Inc.

————. 2009. *Excuses Begone*. Carlsbad: Hay House, Inc.

Ellis, Albert. 1997. *A Guide to Rational Living*. Third edition. Hollywood: Melvin Powers Wilshire Book Company.

Gawain, Shakti. 2000. *Creating True Prosperity*. Novato: Nataraj.

————. 2001. *Developing Intuition*. Novato: Nataraj.

————. 2006. *Creative Visualization*. Novato: Nataraj.

Gilbert, Elizabeth. 2006. *Eat, Pray, Love*. New York: Penguin Books.

Hay, Louise L. 1999. *You Can Heal Your Life*. Carlsbad: Hay House, Inc.

Hillman, James. 1989. *A Blue Fire*. New York: Harper & Row, Publishers.

————. 1996. *The Soul's Code*. New York: Random House.

Holmes, Ernest. 1938. *The Science of Mind*. New York: Jeffery P. Tarcher/Penguin.

————. *Living the Science of Mind*. Camarillo: DeVorss Publications.

————. 2001. *365 Science of Mind*. New York: Jeffery P. Tarcher/Penguin.

Holmes, Ernest and Barker, Raymond Charles. 2006. *365 Days of Richer Living*. Burbank: Science of Mind Publishing.

Houston, Jean. 2012. *The Wizard of Us*. New York/Hillsboro: Atria Books/Beyond Words.

Kidd, Sue Monk. 1990. *When the Heart Waits*. San Francisco: HarperSanFrancisco.

———. 1996. *The Dance of the Dissident Daughter*. San Francisco: HarperSanFrancisco.

Lipton, Bruce H. 2005. *The Biology of Belief*. Carlsbad: Hay House, Inc.

London, Peter. 1989. *No More Secondhand Art*. Boston: Shambhala Publications, Inc.

Markova, Dawna. 1991. *The Art of the Possible*. Boston: Conari Press.

———. 2000. *I Will Not Die an Unlived Life*. Boston: Conari Press.

———. 2008. *Wide Open*. Boston: Conari Press.

Miller, Alice. 1997. *The Drama of the Gifted Child*. New York: Perennial.

Moore, Thomas. 1992. *Care of the Soul*. New York: HarperCollinsPublishers, Inc.

———. 2002. *The Soul's Religion*. New York: HarperCollinsPublishers, Inc.

———. 2008. *A Life at Work*. New York: Broadway Books.

———. 2009. *Writing in the Sand*. Carlsbad: Hay House, Inc.

Muller, Wayne. 1992. *Legacy of the Heart*. New York: Simon & Schuster.

———. *1996. How Then, Shall We Live*. New York: Bantam Books.

———. *2010. A Life of Being, Having, and Doing Enough*. New York: Harmony Books.

Myss, Caroline. 1996. *Anatomy of the Spirit*. New York: Harmony Books.

———. 2003. *Sacred Contracts*. New York: Three Rivers Press.

———. 2013. *Archetypes*. Carlsbad: Hay House, Inc.

Northrup, Dr. Christiane and Schulz, Dr. Mona Lisa. 1999. *Igniting Intuition*. Carlsbad: Hay House Audio.

———. 2001. *Intuitive Listening*. Carlsbad: Hay House Audio.

Oliver, Mary. 1992. *New and Selected Poems Volume One*. Boston: Beacon Press.

Palmer, Parker J. 2000. *Let Your Life Speak*. San Francisco: Josey-Bass.

———. 2004. *A Hidden Wholeness*. San Francisco: Josey-Bass.

Peale, Norman Vincent. 2011. *The Power of Positive Thinking*. New York: Ishi Press International.

Pink, Daniel H. 2006. *A Whole New Mind*. New York: Riverhead Trade/Penguin.

Radmacher, Mary Anne. 2007. *Lean Forward Into Your Life*. San Francisco: Conari Press.

———. 2008. *Live Boldly*. San Francisco: Conari Press.

———. 2011. *Live With Intention*. San Francisco: Conari Press.

Ray, Michael. 2004. *The Highest Goal*. San Francisco: Berrett-Koehler Publishers, Inc.

Richardson, Cheryl. 2005. *The Unmistakable Touch of Grace*. New York: Free Press.

———. 2009. *The Art of Extreme Self-Care*. Carlsbad: Hay House, Inc.

Ruiz, don Miguel. 2012. *The Four Agreements*. San Rafael: Amber-Allen Publishing.

————. 2010. *The Fifth Agreement*. San Rafael: Amber-Allen Publishing.

Schneider, Bruce D. 2000. *Relax, You're Already Perfect*. Manalapan: Ebb/Flow Publishing.

————. 2008. *Energy Leadership*. Hoboken: John Wiley & Sons, Inc.

Sports Fitness Advisor. 2013. "Core Strength Training—Not Just About Your Abs." Sports Fitness Advisor. Accessed March 30. www.sport-fitness-advisor.com/core-strength-training.html.

Teasdale, Sara. 1966. *Collected Poems of Sara Teasdale*. London: Collier-Macmillan Ltd.

The Sense of Smell Lab. 2013. "Unfortunately, We Take Our Sense of Smell for Granted." The Sense of Smell Lab. Accessed January 22. www.thesoslab.com/sense-of-smell.asp.

Whyte, David. 1994. *The Heart Aroused*. New York: Currency Doubleday.

————. 2001. *Crossing the Unknown Sea*. New York: Riverhead Books.

Williamson, Marianne. 1992. *A Return to Love*. New York: Harper Collins Publishers, Inc.

Zander, Rosamund Stone and Zander, Benjamin. 2000. *The Art of Possibility*. New York: Penguin.

Index

CPSIA information can be obtained at www.ICGtesting.com
Printed in the USA
BVOW081457300613

324665BV00003B/4/P